Kindred
Grief Care

GUIDANCE FOR REACHING OUT,
SHOWING UP, AND SUPPORTING LOSS

Francesca Lynn Arnoldy

First edition, 2026
Published by Contemplative Doula
ISBN 978-1-7327806-6-8
FrancescaLynnArnoldy.com

"Grief as 'an expected part of life' belongs to us, as individuals and as part of a society. *Kindred Grief Care* is the handbook for becoming familiar and connecting with grief, whether our own or in presence with another's. In her genuine and profoundly human style, Francesca guides us with reverence and respect for the uniqueness of the grieving process, inviting greater awareness in our communities and offering truly supportive approaches for understanding loss and healing."

–Wilka Roig, death educator and activist

"So many of us struggle with how to show up skillfully for a loved one, friend, or neighbor who is grieving. Take a slow, deep breath and open the pages of *Kindred Grief Care*. This book offers a deeper understanding to the griever, practical tools for any person who genuinely cares, and solace to everyone."

–Dina Stander, end-of-life navigator and founder of the Northeast Death Care Collaborative

"Whether you are a bereavement volunteer, a family member, or you have a chance meeting on the street with a friend experiencing loss, you will find Francesca's insights grounded in understanding and acceptance. There are so many places where I, as a reader, would put page markers or highlight portions of exquisitely worded phrases and strong points. Grief care kindred, known as *students of endings and companions to mourners,* will find this book an invaluable resource."

–Pamela Macpherson, hospice volunteer and author of *Vigil: The Poetry of Presence*

"With *Kindred Grief Care*, Francesca Lynn Arnoldy replicates the nurturing, honest space she creates in her courses. It is full of practical insights, stories, and tools to care for your family, neighbors, and friends as they navigate loss. Francesca asks us to reflect on our personal experiences, and how they may support–or hinder–as we offer a safe landing place to the bereaved. This book is for everyone, from compassionate colleagues to experienced professionals, as they step into the vital role of supporting the grievers in their world."

–Meagan Williams, death doula and educator

"I know Francesca to be a compassionate and insightful human being. Her words guide us with honesty and clarity toward what is brave and generous when the hearts of those we care for are hurting. As I let go of my sense of helplessness, I was reconnected with the sheer power of community to hold one another with love and care during a time of grieving."

–Anika Nailah, author and community builder

"This book continues Arnoldy's ongoing exploration of the shift from sympathy to empathy to compassion, and the discipline required to stay present without trying to 'fix' suffering. She treats compassion as a practice built through steadiness, attunement, and trusting people with the truth of their own experience. She also highlights the role of normalizing—the way it helps grievers make sense of reactions that feel chaotic or contradictory, offering permission to feel what they feel."

–Meredith Parfet, hospice chaplain and crisis management expert

To the *Grief Care Kindred*—the compassionate loved ones, neighbors, and colleagues willing to reach out and show up during times of hardship and heartache: You are the medicine the world needs.

And to Jacques: May it be so.

Contents

Note to Readers

Grief burrows into the uncharted territory of our individual hearts, minds, and bodies. Hence, this guidebook does not claim to be exhaustive or encompassing of all possibilities, because no one can claim to fully *know* another's experience of loss. Terms like "might" and "can" repeat throughout, as there are no guarantees with grief.

The information, examples, and approaches included come from my work as a doula, my research in StoryListening, and a variety of respected sources. Let me be clear, though: I am a student of mortality and endings, not an all-knowing expert. These are spaces within which I practice and study. This guidebook contains the best of what I have learned so far—the poignant lessons that have encouraged my awareness, courage, and healing.

Will it speak to every broken heart enduring any type of loss? Possibly not, as there are infinite causes and expressions of grief. Yet, I hope some of what is shared will align and resonate with each reader.

The main goals of this book are to (1) strengthen our communal fluency and understanding of grief, and (2) bolster your confidence to support friends, neighbors, colleagues, and family members through complex transitions. The aim of any artistic creation is to incite an emotional response, so whatever this guidebook stirs within you, may you find the curiosity to turn inward and reflect deeply.

- No generative artificial intelligence (AI) was used to outline or draft this book.

- *They* is used as a plural and singular pronoun for ease and inclusion.

- The term *kindred* is used in its colloquial form as an adjective as well as in its more ancient form as a noun to describe caring community members connected to others through affinity.

Kindred (n.) c. 1200, perhaps late Old English, *kinraden,* "family, lineage; race, nation, tribe, people; kinsfolk, blood relations" (Etymonline, s.v. "kindred").

Foreword

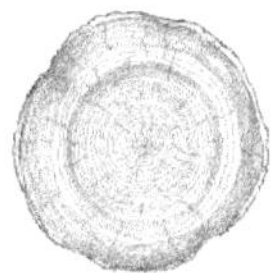

Every few months, my husband sought reassurance from his oncologist that all was proceeding as expected. He would ask, "How long do you think I have left?" and the doctor would respond with a patient smile. "Even though you've surpassed your shelf life, you're doing remarkably well."

There are few callings more courageous—or more sacred—than choosing to support others through life's final stages and in the aftermath of loss. I believe my husband exceeded all prognoses for a decade through a combination of science, technology, hope, and the wisdom of deathcare practitioners.

Despite the growing body of knowledge surrounding death and dying, few of us are equipped to respond authentically to loss as it unfolds. I came to understand this from the inside out—as the bereaved. In the many months of profound and disorienting grief that followed, I learned that not all well-intentioned words of sympathy or gestures of support bring genuine comfort.

I first became aware of Francesca Lynn Arnoldy through colleagues who had studied doula practices and thanatology with her. When the opportunity arose, I was delighted to invite her to record an *Exit Interview* podcast for Bevival. However, it was not until several months later that the true depth of her work revealed itself—through a simple email message. Her gentle inquiry met me where I was, allowing space to share or to remain silent. What began as a few brief exchanges quietly companioned me through my healing. Then, as the fog of grief began to lift, Francesca asked if I might be interested in reading her forthcoming guide.

What you hold in your hands is the embodiment of that wisdom. This work offers a deeply informed framework for tending to the spaces shaped by sorrow. Whether you approach these pages as a caregiver, a healthcare professional, or one drawn by compassion to serve, you will find here a synthesis of practical guidance and empathic insight that reflects why Francesca's voice is so vital in the evolving landscape of death literacy.

Caren Martineau
Founder, Bevival.com
Where Death Literacy Lives

1

Beginnings

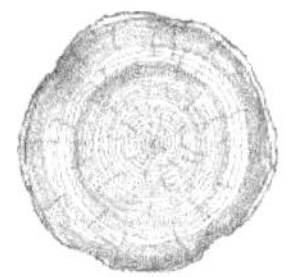

Loss, like love, is part of life. Whether we're mourning the death of a person or pet, or we're facing a different sort of transition, endings infiltrate our existence. It's in our nature to grieve the times and connections that have held meaning. It's also in our nature to feel concerned when those around us experience grief.

Every type of loss deserves acknowledgement and support. We are often hesitant to step into such intense moments, though, for fear of saying the wrong thing and making the anguish worse. But that's why you're here—to learn effective methods for offering compassionate condolences and care.

Even after years of study and practice, entering someone else's grief space still gives me pause—as it should. Whether I'm in the role of a hospice volunteer, doula, loved one, or community member,

I recognize the weight of the moment. Grief thickens the air around loss, and it's difficult to wade through.

Test of Courage

During a memorable shift at our local hospice home, I went to check on a resident in need of vigil planning (meaning coordinating volunteers to be at the bedside during his final hours). As I entered, I quietly knocked and announced my presence. It was immediately apparent that this resident wouldn't be able to respond. He was actively dying.

I checked with the nurse to see if he had requested privacy. He hadn't, so I pulled up a chair next to his bed. I sat quietly with him until a visitor arrived. Then, the energy shifted—in the room and within me. I wondered, "What's the dynamic between these two? Will I be an intrusion or a welcome presence?"

I introduced myself and learned that the visitor was his adult son. He seemed relieved to have another person there, so I decided to stay. My nerves fluttered. I didn't know how this time would go. I wasn't sure what would be needed, and I didn't know what I should offer. It turns out, at least for me, that it's more straightforward and comfortable to sit with a dying person than it is to sit with someone facing loss. But I've learned how to work with my worries and recognize them as reverence for uncertain realms.

The son asked about his father's status. I noted what I'd been observing—peaceful yet infrequent breathing while he slept soundly. As the son put down his belongings, he explained his predicament.

"I've been here for almost two weeks," he started. "I came as soon as I heard the end was near. I wanted to be here, of course—I *need* to be here—but no one can tell me how much longer it'll take. That sounds cold, I know, but I can only be away from my job and my family for so long. I'm torn. I want to be here for my dad, but I also need to get home. I don't know what to do." He shook his head, sadness hanging heavily on his shoulders.

Hand on my heart, I responded, "That sounds really hard." I paused to allow for silence to follow my gesture of concern.

"I'm feeling pulled and guilty no matter where I am right now," he continued, making his way over to the bed. "He's been sleeping like this for days. The nurses keep saying it could be any minute."

"Everyone's experience is so unique. It's hard to know for sure," I confirmed.

As he gazed toward his father, an idea came to mind. Although I didn't want to prescribe a solution, I did want to make space for him to find a way through this dilemma.

"Why don't you tell me about your dad, and I'll take down notes for the team? That way, if you do have to leave, we'll know him even better and we'll be clear on any wishes you might have for his care."

He agreed, so I asked questions about his father's life and personality. From across the bed, he gingerly held his dad's hand while speaking of memories and quirks, chuckling at some moments and sighing through others. I asked about preferences in music, books, poetry, and prayers.

Lastly, I asked if there were any words he'd want spoken in his absence—any comforting phrases or messages we could repeat. He took his time, thinking. He kissed the back of his dad's hand and then cleared his throat.

"I want him to know it's okay. He's been sick for so long, and he's suffered so much. I just want him to be at peace. We love him. I'll miss him for sure, but we'll be okay. The family will be okay."

A slow exhale and nod of his head let me know he was done sharing. I thanked him. Not only did I gather valuable information to relay to team members, but this son had the chance to say what was on his mind and in his heart. As someone who works in deathcare, I've seen how unspoken words can weigh down a mourner. In the end, he stayed for a while longer and then said his final farewell.

Did our talk save him from grieving? No, but that was never the goal. Did it give him a measure of comfort and closure while alleviating some guilt? I hope so. Did it become a lasting memory of his father's dying journey? Undoubtedly, yes, filtered through his own distinct lens.

Grief Care Kindred

Although loss is an inevitable part of life, grief is complex. Witnessing pain is difficult. And knowing what to say or do is challenging, which keeps many people away. But, we are interdependent beings. In *No Future Without Forgiveness,* Desmond Tutu writes, "My humanity is bound up in yours, for we can only be human together."[1]

This is the depth of awareness we hold as those who support neighbors and loved ones through times of transition. As grief care kindred, we don't say, "Follow me. I know the way." Instead, we make room for the unknown, creating openings for discovery. We trust the compass within each of us, even when it seems out of reach. And we acknowledge how much courage and patience healing requires.

Providing kindred grief care is not a job or formal role; it's part of being a warmhearted community member. It is compassion embodied. When those around us face loss, we feel compelled to show up and step in to offer companionship.

How can we cultivate this kind of willingness and then convey it to those in need? Throughout the pages of this guidebook, you'll find tried-and-true techniques along with explanations of how to skillfully apply them.

Why is this topic so important to study? For societies to thrive, people must gather together—not only for celebrations, but for times of heartbreak, as well. We need to remember we're not meant to suffer in isolation and recognize that connection can be an antidote to despair. The supportive actions we'll discuss, which encourage this togetherness, benefit both the receiver *and* the provider, often leading to a meaningful sense of purpose.

We'll begin by building a solid foundation of knowledge and a shared vocabulary. Next, we'll cover best practices for phrasing condolences and creating conditions that promote healing. Then, we'll discuss specialized approaches to listening as well as connectional care. If time is limited and you need to prepare quickly, read "Foundational Knowledge" and "Grief Visits" before returning to the rest.

As we review concepts, we'll shift our focus between developing an effective mindset and meeting the needs of individual mourners. By the end of the book, you'll be more prepared to customize your words and offerings for different situations with increased courage and humility.

The Pathway to Kindred Grief Care

1. Study loss and grief healing.

2. Learn directly from those you support.

3. Nurture your heart and keep connected to the humanity within you.

2

Foundational Knowledge

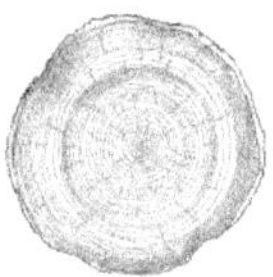

In *We Bereaved*, a moving collection of poetic essays, Helen Keller describes the resilience of the human spirit and the universality of grief.

> We bereaved are not alone. We belong to the largest company in all the world—the company of those who have known suffering. When it seems that our sorrow is too great to be borne, let us think of the great family of the heavy-hearted into which our grief has given us entrance, and, inevitably, we will feel about us their arms, their sympathy, their understanding.[2]

We are not alone in the experience of loss, nor are we meant to be. Grief is universal, and yet types of loss vary, as do individual interpretations. Throughout this guidebook, we will aim to honor grief as a part of life—challenging and unbidden as it can be—and discuss strategies for supporting the *heavy-hearted*.

First though, let's develop a common language for our discussion.

Grief Literacy

Although there are many theories and definitions of grief—some disputed, others respected—endings are only truly understood by actually experiencing them. Grief becomes *known* to us by thinking and feeling our way through it—by struggling at moments and gradually integrating the resulting changes. Still, explanations of experiences are useful. Frameworks can help us build an understanding and vocabulary.

"Grief literacy" means having an awareness of how people face and navigate loss, and an understanding of the related systems of care available to the bereaved. It means being informed and resourceful. A person with increased grief literacy is better prepared to provide emotional and informational support.

In service of being informed, let's discuss some relevant definitions. Specific wording varies somewhat from source to source, but our goal is to summarize prevailing themes. Let's start with grief, bereavement, and mourning.

Simply put, **grief** is a natural response to a significant loss or transition. Significance is subjective, of course, and each person experiences and expresses grief in their own way. Most often, we think of grief as an emotional reaction, but loss can affect people socially, psychologically, physically, spiritually, and mentally as well.

A loss can be a death, but it can also be the end of a relationship, career, identity, home location, or future dream. Or it might be a change in stability or independence, the close of an era, receiving a difficult diagnosis or news of infertility, or another profound shift, like becoming an "empty nester" when adult children move away. Some people describe "big D" or "little d" *death*, or similarly "big L" or "little l" *loss* to distinguish major and more minor examples.

Bereavement is the time period of grief following a loss. Although it's not universally agreed upon, this span is often considered the initial weeks or months. Sometimes sources and care providers refer to a full year of bereavement in order to include the first passing of every holiday and anniversary. There's also the administrative term "bereavement leave" that describes any time off an employee is allowed, which may or may not be paid.

Mourning is the outward expression of grief, either individual or collective. This can include emotional releases like crying or anger outbursts as well as wearing certain clothing or jewelry to signify loss. Commemorative ceremonies, like funerals or the building of a memorial bench, are part of mourning.

We'll be using these terms fairly interchangeably as we reference grieving people as "mourners" or "the bereaved."

In the appendix, there are detailed descriptions of different kinds of grief. Review and return to them as needed. What's most important to understand, though, is that loss takes many forms. To appreciate the complexities within varied endings, we need to suspend judgment and any urge to categorize them as more or less worthy of care.

Compassionate Condolences

The words we use have an impact. While they don't need to be perfect, we can aim for them to be thoughtful and supportive. Specific phrases related to grief will land differently, so there's no one right way to offer condolences. There is one rather wrong way, though, and that is to say nothing at all—as in, not acknowledging the loss whatsoever.

Unsurprisingly, people are commonly nervous to "say the wrong thing" and "make it worse" when someone is already distressed. How can we mindfully choose our wording? Here are options that are generally safe to use, adapted from Grief.com:[3]

Phrasing to Use:

- "What a [heartbreak, shock, tragedy, deep loss]," followed by invitational silence.

- "I wish I had the right words—just please know I care."

- "I can't claim to know exactly how you feel or what you're going through, but I'm here to listen."

- "You and your loved one are in my [thoughts, prayers, heart]."

- "Can I share a favorite memory of…?"

- Offer a hug or a hand to hold instead.

- Offer to help with a specific task, like groceries or dependent care.

- Simply be with the person and continue to reach out.

These suggestions aren't necessarily universally applicable. You will need to filter any messaging and actions through what seems natural and suits the dynamic you share with the mourner. To bolster your courage, hold the intention that you are (1) honoring their loss and (2) being kind. This becomes the groundwork for all your offerings, including those that are verbal.

There are ways that words can be harmful, though, and this usually happens without full awareness. When I lead workshops on grief, without fail, participants share examples of hurtful statements said to them when they were bereaved. They recall the words vividly, even when voiced long ago. Most often, the messages included either telling the grieving person how to feel, what to do, or what their loss meant. Here are examples of what to avoid, adapted from Grief.com:[4]

Phrasing to Avoid:

- Minimizing: "At least [your person lived a long life, is out of pain, isn't suffering anymore]."

- Attributing meaning: "Everything happens for a reason," or "They're in a better place."

- Questioning: "Aren't you over it yet?"

- Making assumptions: "I know how you feel," or "I know how painful this loss is."

- Providing solutions: "You can get pregnant again/get another pet."

- Providing reasons: "He did what he came here to do, and it was his time," or "She was such a good person, [higher power, realm of afterlife] called her home."

- Providing direction: "Be strong/positive," or "You should/I would…"

Some of the previous examples are more obviously thoughtless ("Aren't you over it yet?") while others sound more benign. That's because there might be some truth to them sometimes for some people. Please remember, though, honesty isn't necessarily supportive; it can actually be undermining and insensitive. While a mourner might, in theory, be able to become pregnant again or get another pet, that isn't thoughtful to point out, as it fails to address their current grief.

Assigning meaning to someone else's experience is not empowering, and neither is imposing your personal belief system. What's generally needed is ample time and opportunity for the mourner to come to their own realizations as they try to make sense of what happened and begin to heal. If a grieving person shares their own theories or conclusions, you can mirror them back, strengthening their effect.

If you're ever at a loss for words, don't be afraid to admit it. It's a sign of humility. As bereaved mother and grief coach Terri Chaplin states, "Grief isn't meant to be explained away. Sometimes all we need is for someone to sit with us in the pain."[5]

Grief Effects

Grief can be very intense, especially during the initial days and weeks following a profound loss. Many people feel crushed, destroyed, or even *undone*. It can seem as though their world is ending.

While it's assumed grief can wreak havoc on feelings, it can also affect other bodily functions, like eating habits and sleep routines, and cause headaches, fatigue, increased heart rate, and stomach pain. According to the Eluna Network, grief is also associated with brain fog, spiraling thoughts, flashbacks, forgetfulness, irritability, withdrawal from hobbies and social activities, escapism with substances or distractions, and existential worry.[6] Whatever the cause, grief can infiltrate all aspects of a person's being.

Mourners might also shift between seemingly opposing sensations. They could feel deep sorrow and also solace that any suffering has ended, or weighty guilt and also pride regarding caregiving or surrogate decision-making. Or they might be bereft one moment and in disbelief the next.

An abrupt ending has the potential to call into question everything that a person has valued and thought to be true. On the contrary, it can solidify spiritual or religious beliefs. Although contrasting emotions aren't actually in conflict—because they can exist simultaneously—they can create inner turmoil. There's a broad spectrum of potential reactions. Most mourners experience a messy mix.

Grief Dynamics

Specific circumstances influence a person's grieving process. For instance, with a death loss, if the relationship with the dying person had been conflicted (perhaps because of neglect, estrangement, or mistreatment), then the mourner may experience more complicated reactions. This might include an unwelcome return to difficult memories from the past. There might also be a sense of relief that no additional pain can be inflicted. And the mourner sometimes longs for a resolution that's no longer possible or for a healthier relationship that "could have been."

This kind of grief can manifest as bitterness, sadness, or even rage toward an injustice that can't be rectified. The healing process often involves sharing pent-up feelings aloud, which can be challenging due to the common ethos that "we shouldn't speak ill of the deceased." Healthy grieving is rooted in emotional honesty, though, and releasing complex thoughts and feelings can be vital to integrating loss.

If, conversely, the dynamics were healthy and loving, the loss might be more acknowledged by society and straightforward in terms of how it's "supposed" to present. Yet this depth of grief can be more intense than expected. The following lines from the television show *1883*, delivered by Shea Brennan (played by Sam Elliott), aptly describe heartbreak:

> An Apache scout told me once that when you love somebody, you trade souls with them. They get a piece of yours, and you get a piece of theirs. But when your love dies, a little piece of you dies with them. That's why you hurt so bad.[7]

When people love each other within a close relationship, they share a lot of themselves. They carry the other person's voice and imprint inside of them, and vice versa. Their very personhood—the way they understand themselves and the world—is woven together with the other person's. When a cherished beloved dies, especially one who has shared the bulk of someone's days and affection, the absence of their presence is profound.

In *The Wild Edge of Sorrow*, author and psychotherapist Francis Weller explains, "My grief says that I dared to love, that I allowed another to enter the very core of my being and find a home in my heart."[8] In a similarly moving way, writer Jamie Anderson describes grief as *love*. "It's all the love you want to give but cannot. All that unspent love gathers up in the corners of your eyes, the lump in your throat, and in that hollow part of your chest. Grief is just love with no place to go."[9]

Hierarchy of Loss

It's crucial to avoid comparing or ranking losses. While it's true that some endings can feel cataclysmic while others seem more manageable, loss is not a competition. No one should have to justify their pain to receive support. We must recognize that individual responses vary as they result from the attachment forged to what or who is gone as well as learned behavior, messaging, coping techniques or lack thereof, along with layers of lived experience that can either facilitate or interfere with the healing process.

In the end, grief is grief. Loss is loss. And the bereaved deserve kindness and understanding. That is what we offer as grief care kindred.

3

The Role of Grief Care Kindred

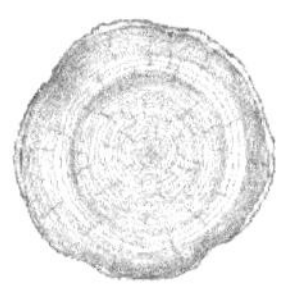

Before discussing who we are as grief care kindred, let's clarify who we are not. When taking on this role within our communities, we are not operating in a clinical capacity. While mental health counseling and support groups can be invaluable—and sometimes necessary—in a person's journey, kindred grief care is a separate strand of the care web.

It's crucial that non-clinical people remain as such and defer to professionals as needed. While we do not supply medical or psychological treatment or advice as grief care kindred, we can become a bridge to clinical services. Honoring roles and scopes of care helps keep people safe.

So, who *are* grief care kindred? We are the neighbors, colleagues, and loved ones who reach out and show up when someone is down. We cultivate a presence of compassion, patience, and trust in the face of turmoil and overwhelm. When stress and anxiety escalate, we become even more calm.

What's needed to provide kindred grief care is (1) a brave willingness rooted in earnest concern for the wellbeing of others, and (2) some specialized techniques for providing support. These techniques, which we will cover, are essential because they benefit and protect both the giver and receiver of care. Our next step is to turn inward to identify and examine core motivations for wanting to take on this role.

Inner Purpose

Sometimes individuals yearn to be the kind of support they didn't have access to during a past heartbreak. They are motivated to become what was lacking, embodying what they wish had been available. Alternatively, when someone felt abundantly cared for during an intense period, they might want to become the presence they appreciated by emulating what was offered. Lastly, people might have witnessed what they perceive to be beneficial and thoughtful during someone else's experience and thus set out to adopt those practices.

Pause and Reflect

To foster clarity, spend time exploring the impulse behind your efforts. Using your preferred tool for introspection—whether it's closing your eyes and thinking deeply, contemplating while taking a walk, or creatively expressing ideas through writing or art—answer the following questions before continuing in the guidebook. Allow insights to emerge without judging them. Be honest and open to get the most out of this exercise.

1. What motivates you to support a person facing loss?

2. What losses from the past influence your current interest?

3. What might you be attempting to avoid or replicate in this role?

How did it feel to reflect on your inner reasoning for wanting to provide kindred grief care? Did you try to dissuade or convince yourself of a certain truth, or were you able to be neutral and simply observe?

Providing skillful emotional support requires patience, awareness, and understanding, not only of loss but also of yourself. Most of us are *natural nurturers*. We have an inclination toward "pro-social behavior," meaning that we take action to provide comfort and care to those requiring it.

According to educator and author Kendra Cherry, pro-social behaviors are compelled by either (1) egoistic motives, as in improving one's own sense of self; (2) reciprocal benefits, as in expecting a favor to be returned in the future; or (3) altruistic reasons, as in acting purely out of concern for another individual.[10] These motivations point to the need for additional exploration. We'll continue to work with them, as they have the potential to shift from internal incentives to an unconscious agenda.

Arguably, the purest form of care comes from altruism. These efforts are quieter. They require no applause or appreciation, as they are powered by heartfelt compassion. They are *pure* because there are no expectations attached. Altruistic supporters arrive ready and open. If their presence isn't accepted, no offense is taken. Instead, they silently celebrate that the griever is voicing their needs and take comfort in knowing their willingness to visit has been conveyed.

Actions completely devoid of ego aren't terribly common, however. We're human. We carry our own personal losses and unhealed wounds. And we have hopes for others, notably that they will heal and re-engage with life in meaningful ways after a loss. All this is natural. Self-awareness is key, as is examining any hidden influences.

Agenda Check

Before entering into someone's time of hardship, first pause and ask: How is this person's loss affecting me? What is it bringing up? What am I bringing to this visit in terms of my own *stuff*? What might I need to address ahead of time and process afterward?

Physician and author Rachel Naomi Remen explains tending to others in this way:

> Helping, fixing, and serving represent three different ways of seeing life. When you help, you see life as weak. When you fix, you see life as broken. When you serve, you see life as whole. Fixing and helping may be the work of the ego, and service the work of the soul.[11]

How can we be sure we're serving versus helping or fixing? One important step is to move from sympathy to empathy to compassion—a necessary pathway to providing sustainable, person-centered care. In my work and writing, I return to this trajectory again and again as a guiding "north star." It is not a contemplation that you can complete; it is one to revisit regularly with an openness to learn more.

Cultivating Compassion

In the pathway toward embodied compassion, both sympathy and empathy are valuable stepping stones. To begin with, sympathy is feeling sadness in response to someone's difficult situation. When we recognize a person is suffering, our hearts sink in response. A wave of heaviness washes over us. When we enter into a conversation or visit from a place of sympathy, our emotions can easily become muddled with those of the mourners. And we tend to carry the weight of the interaction long after it ends.

Empathy is the act of trying to feel what someone else is feeling, whether it's deep sadness, anxiety, relief, self-doubt, or any other emotion. When we care from a place of empathy, we attempt to mirror and match an experience that's not actually ours. Thus, we might try to relate by sharing our own stories of loss, which can shrink the mourner's space for processing. Or we might try to envision going through the other person's grief, which can be taxing. Again, this is a beneficial step to take and to also move beyond, as sympathy and empathy can exhaust our energy levels.

Sympathy and empathy align with helping and fixing as previously described. The support person wants to resolve any pain others are enduring as well as any secondary suffering they themselves have absorbed. As a result, the supporter often becomes more directive, giving advice or instructions for how to reach the "other side" of grief—to "get over it." There's a wish for the bereaved to hurry up and get better, so things can be stable, and life can get "back to normal" as soon as possible.

Compassion aligns more with serving. With this approach, we slow down and learn directly from the person grieving. We observe and honor how they are feeling and what they might need from us. As grief care kindred, we hold the recognition of our own emotions—past and current—quietly in the background to allow ample opportunity for the mourner to feel their way through loss.

An orientation of compassion is empowering as grief care kindred hold a steady belief in people's inner wisdom and strength. We trust mourners with their grief, knowing there will likely be moments of doubt and overwhelm. In response, we act as supportive witnesses to both their pain and healing. It's a more sustainable approach because we are better able to maintain our wellness and energy. We know it is a privilege to be allowed into such vulnerability.

The Latin roots of "compassion" translate to "suffer with," but we need to do so with great care. While all mortal beings struggle with impermanence and endings, as these are universal themes of our human experience, we also recognize the uniqueness of each person's journey. This understanding of compassion will naturally inspire consideration, connection, and community.

Avoiding Assumptions

Grief care kindred are other-oriented and non-directive. Instead of imagining how we would want to receive care, which would be rooted in empathy, we take cues from the bereaved. We learn directly from them while providing personalized support. Our approach centers on humility and respect.

This means working to identify what is ours versus what belongs to someone else, whether regarding beliefs, preferences, or expressions of grief. This effort to determine our own "stuff" is unending because we continuously evolve. The following three steps help foster understanding.

1. Introspection

    Deepen your clarity about your own identity, perspectives, culture, heritage, conditioning, belief system, biases, and grief experiences.

2. Respectful Inquiry

    Even when you learn a facet of someone's identity or background—for example, their race, ethnicity, religion, gender, disability status, etc.—you don't automatically know what it *means* to them and for them. After building rapport, you might ask or discern: "How can I honor or support this part of who you are?"

3. Awareness

Some parts of an individual's personhood are less visible yet are essential. Some examples are a person's sexual orientation, whether they're adopted, or if they're neurodiverse. These less obvious identities are often only revealed within a truly trusting relationship.

Pause and Reflect

Part of approaching grief care from a place of compassion is trying to assess and understand what is *yours*. In service of that, contemplate the following prompts.

Think back to a time you received support following a loss or major life transition. If it feels safe to do so, return to the experience and recall as many details as possible. If that's too consuming, focus on the support itself instead of the reason for it. What words or offerings landed well? What approaches didn't resonate? Consider where they came from and what they were trying to accomplish. What ended up being most comforting to you?

Once you've journaled or thought deeply, acknowledge the distinctiveness of your specific answers. What brought you solace might differ from others. We each have our own ways of recovering from hardship.

In workshops, when I ask these questions about receiving support, there are common themes in the answers. People cite the following as most beneficial:

- Having the opportunity to talk about their experience openly.

- Having a steady, kind presence available.

They often say they yearned to still feel like themselves and to have their suffering witnessed. They appreciated sharing their thoughts and having their experiences validated. Healing can deepen when people draw together. Connection and comfort are not always guaranteed during trying times, though.

Loneliness

Loss can lead to alienation. This can happen on multiple levels. First, a mourner misses what or who is gone. There's a void. This can create longing as well as loneliness. Second, grieving can seem like a solitary process because no one can fully venture into the depths of what another is undergoing. There can be similarities when people grieve a shared loss together, yet there are always some differences. Third, mourners might avoid social interactions, fearing they're not stable enough to "hold it together" or because they simply don't have the energy. Lastly, friends, neighbors, and colleagues sometimes shy away from the bereaved.

All told, loss can be a recipe for loneliness. As grief care kindred, we don't visit in order to rescue someone from their experience. We're there so people don't feel quite so alone in it. We keep them company and acknowledge their emotions while normalizing the unruly nature of grief. People are free to mourn in our presence. They don't need to stifle or conceal their reactions or worries.

Normalizing

When it comes to loss, we know it's a universal experience, yet we can never say "never" and never say "always" when describing it. There's no one passageway through grief, but there are some commonalities that can help a mourner build trust in the process. As a doula and hospice volunteer, I have found *normalizing* to be an effective approach.

Instead of thinking about "normal" versus "abnormal," which might alienate a grieving person further, we can reference what is *natural* or *common*. In my work, I use phrasing like, "It's not uncommon for people grieving to [feel lost, question everything, worry about the future]." I might also point out, "It's natural to react that way following a loss."

As we continue to cover these topics throughout this guidebook, you'll broaden your frame of reference and strengthen your ability to normalize when needed. Each time you visit a grieving person, you'll learn more. And these "lessons" will continue to shape and expand your perspective and increase your understanding.

Building a Base

Reflecting on the knowledge you've developed about inner motivations, compassion, and loneliness, let's now discuss how to establish a sturdy base for grief care. When a person is feeling vulnerable after a loss, they might become more impressionable and overly trusting. Or they might become excessively doubtful and cynical. These extremes arise because a significant loss changes everything a person has known to be real and reliable about life. They're left with uncertainty—and that is a wobbly base. In response, we can work to build a more secure one.

Secure attachments are crucial for healthy development during infancy, but also throughout adulthood. Looking to attachment-based theories for inspiration, grief care kindred can become a "secure base." Developmental psychologist Mary Ainsworth explains that security formed with an attachment figure provides stability and safety in moments of stress.[12] This kind of attachment doesn't need to be long-term to be effective, though. My doula work has repeatedly affirmed this, as I generally provide care to clients for limited periods of months, weeks, days, or just hours.

As a birth doula, I have shown up a few times as a stranger during labor when filling in as the emergency backup option. The client would be in the throes of contractions, and I would quickly work to earn their trust and determine what kind of support would be most fitting. I'd offer attentiveness and encouragement, holding love in my heart for their struggles and celebrations. I became a steady, secure "base" while maintaining a belief in them and the birthing process itself, as they vacillated between exhaustion and excitement, frustration and hope.

Our effort is similar within the realm of loss. By embodying trust and patience, grief care kindred can become a secure base. This steadiness is invaluable when all else feels upside down. A mourner can feel safe to struggle and even fall apart while being *held* with trusting kindness.

Grief Support Avatar

People regularly describe grief using metaphors. It's a rollercoaster of emotion, a dark cloud, a heavy weight, or a stormy sea. What sort of symbolic object or figure could you represent within such turbulent scenarios? Perhaps you could envision yourself as the sun, ever-present above the cloud line, or as a well-rooted tree that sways in strong winds without upending. Or you could picture yourself as a buoy that never drifts away, no matter the intensity of the waves, or as a lighthouse that rhythmically sends signals of safety.

Pause and Reflect

Take a moment to brainstorm a grief care avatar for yourself. This practice can help you step into the role more fully and infuse calm compassion. Keep in mind the goal of each mourner feeling secure in your presence. You'll cultivate a space within and around you that feels homelike and soothing, like a refuge. This way, those reeling from loss might find more courage to gradually immerse themselves into their grief to access healing.

4

Conditions for Healing

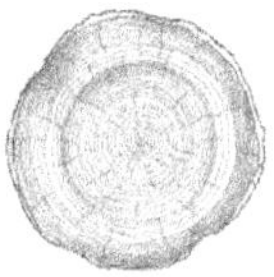

As grief care kindred, our overarching intention is to help create conditions that foster healing. The catch is, each mourner requires their own specialized conditions, and we can't automatically know what they are. Loss looks, sounds, and feels different for every person each time they're bereaved.

Optimal conditions promote a person's ability to grieve fully—to do the emotional and practical work of processing an ending and adapting to a new version of life. With adequate support, mourners can tap into a budding belief that they have what's needed, inside and around them. Then, they might build more trust in their own capacity to navigate and endure such trying terrain.

Grief Healing

A significant loss is meant to be felt, expressed, held, and *metabolized*—that is, emotionally digested and moved through a person's system. It might even be alchemized into a renewed sense of purpose or passion for life. Grief is not meant to be wholly bypassed, solved, or controlled, although periods of respite are part of the process.

Healing is dynamic and rhythmic. The bereaved sometimes step closer to the reality of their loss and all it means for the rest of life. Other times, they step farther away from the epicenter, instead choosing to focus on diversions or regular responsibilities.

In 1999, researchers Margaret Stroebe and Henk Schut introduced their theory, "The Dual Process Model of Coping with Bereavement," to describe how a mourner's focus shifts between loss-oriented stressors and restoration-oriented stressors.[13] In other words, people cycle between confronting their loss and trying to return to a "normal" existence. Since grieving can be exhausting, taking breaks is necessary. This kind of *grief dosing* is natural and healthy.

The Main Elements of Grief Healing

1. Leaning into Loss

2. Leaning into Life

3. Resting

Within these three overarching categories, there are a variety of more specific efforts or tasks that call to a grieving person at different times. They depend on an individual's temperament, personality, and the circumstances of their experience.

Common Grief Healing Needs

- To Feel and Express Grief

Untamed grief can be intense and might include sobbing, wailing, or screaming. It can also look like a quieter kind of sadness or even laughter at the absurdity of what seems impossible to accept. Frustration and anxiety are sometimes present and might need to be released. A mourner might feel relief that any suffering has ended after a death preceded by a serious illness and then guilt about that relief. Seemingly contradictory, wide-ranging emotions are not uncommon.

- To Commemorate Loss

Some people observe religious, spiritual, or cultural traditions to honor their grief. The structure and familiarity of long-established rituals can be comforting during times of upheaval. Other individuals incorporate inspiration from various sources to create their own commemoration.

People grieving might wear shirts featuring a photograph of the deceased or have custom bumper stickers made with the name of their beloved along with their birth and death dates. Some mourners get memorial tattoos while others have special keepsakes made, like jewelry containing cremains or teddy bears sewn from their person's favorite clothing. Creating altars or shrines with photographs, small belongings, candles, and other mementos connected to the loss is a common practice.

- To Find a Distraction

When focusing on grief becomes too draining, a mourner might need to turn away temporarily. This could include taking a nap, cooking or baking, watching a funny movie, exercising, or reading a book. Any activity that can hold their focus for even just a short while can offer a reprieve. These distractions also welcome the bereaved back into living life. They're beginning to see themselves continuing to function—somehow, someway. It's not uncommon for grief to be reactivated during even the most neutral activity, especially initially.

Please note: There's a difference between taking a break from loss and avoiding it entirely. Whether a mourner is entrenched in magical thinking ("my person will return") or they're attempting to numb out completely with substances, blocking grief can be detrimental to their wellbeing. Those grieving cannot evade significant loss and return to "regular life" as though nothing has happened without potential repercussions, like mental or physical health issues. Stifling emotion isn't an effective long-term fix, yet moments, or even phases, of avoidance are common.

- To Carry on with Life

Life keeps on *life-ing*, even after loss. Bills still need to be paid, homes still need to be cleaned, and dependents still need care. Additionally, settling the affairs of the deceased can be a demanding, time-consuming task, depending on how much had been prepared and organized in advance. Sometimes those duties are a welcome distraction. At other times, they are exhausting. Fluctuating reactions are common.

- To Reminisce and Reflect

Remembering life before loss can sometimes be too intense when grief wounds are very tender. Gradually, though, a mourner might want to return to special moments and talk about them, even if it means they'll feel sad. In terms of death losses, strong bonds can endure beyond endings. If an individual loved someone during life, that love doesn't end with death. The emerging silence and absence can be heartbreaking, though, as can lingering regrets, including any harsh words spoken or caring ones left unsaid. Pining for the past and wishing away the new reality is common.

- To Question

Someone experiencing deep grief might question everything as their mind attempts to reconcile a profound shift. The question "How can this be?" repeats and repeats. Mourners might doubt what has happened and what is real, as well as their ability to survive it all. They might wonder about the meaning of life and what happens after death. Grief makes for shaky ground. Rumination is common as the brain needs time and practice to adapt to new realities, roles, and routines.

- To Consider the Future

As a grieving person acknowledges and incorporates loss, they might start to look toward the future, gazing ahead with apathy, disbelief, or curiosity. They might feel hopeful at times, and resistant at others. It's quite common for someone to move closer to the truth of their situation, and then back away again as they consider all that has changed and who they are becoming as a result.

Common Ground

These various responses are appropriate, reasonable, and part of the grief process. Sometimes people need relief. Other times they need release. Sometimes, people need to catch their breath and rest.

How can we know what mourners are seeking, considering they might not even know themselves? We can rely on the guidance of our hearts and the trusted techniques within this book. Here's a look back (and ahead) at some of our key principles.

1. Cultivate a foundation of compassion: We are accessible and trusting.

2. Become a secure base: We are calm and centered.

3. Create attunement: We are attentive and receptive.

Creating Attunement

When attuned to someone, we are fully present and focused on their words, body language, and needs. We notice subtle cues and subtext. Within their grief space, we are sensitive and responsive.

Our primary question as grief care kindred is: Does the mourner need to lean into the loss at this moment or turn away from it? The answer might change day-to-day or even moment-to-moment. In response, we need to be nimble and flexible. If we repeat this question as an informative mantra, it will advise our words and actions in real time. Once we have a sense of the answer, we can offer either direct or indirect support.

In Practice

Leaning into loss could mean the mourner wants to talk about their experience. In response, you will become an attentive listener. Or *leaning into loss* could mean sorting through belongings from a time gone past or creating a remembrance project. Your next question would then be: Do they want company in this task? If so, you can lend a hand. If they, instead, want to be cocooned and protected in the privacy of an effort, your support might be more indirect.

Let's say, for example, the grieving person wants to disperse treasured belongings of their deceased. They plan to choose pieces for loved ones and add a special note with each gift. This task will probably be demanding, exhausting, and maybe even cathartic.

You might ask if they'd like to get started and offer to help. In this scenario, you would *companion* them through the process while gently encouraging their efforts. You would not provide instructions; you would provide presence and assistance. While remembering that grief can lead people to question everything, you can normalize moments of struggle, letting them know it's natural to be indecisive.

Or your support might not be so direct. Maybe the mourner laments they would like to start the task, but they have too many other demands. You might respond, "Sorting through these belongings sounds really important. What can I take off your plate so you can focus on it?" If they have trouble coming up with specific tasks, suggest a few. Maybe you can wash the dishes and bring mail to the post office. Or you can get groceries and take their dog for a walk.

What if a bereaved person seems to be holding back tears or apologizes for being "too emotional"? In response, you can acknowledge the common need to express grief by saying, "Feel free to have a good cry. It's a healthy part of grieving." They might be comfortable doing so in front of you or prefer more privacy. Gently ask and respond accordingly.

Remember, healing takes energy. Center this when checking in and offering care. People will vacillate between leaning into loss and turning away from it. In response, you can either lean in as well or consider how you might lift a burden, so they can spend more time and energy on their process. Even though we are non-directive in our role, giving mourners permission to grieve in *their* own way can be affirming.

Returning to our list of "Common Grief Healing Needs," consider your role within those different situations. If a mourner is expressing grief, how might you respond? If a mourner is seeking a distraction, what could you offer? If a mourner needs to complete regular tasks of living, how might you be helpful?

If a mourner wants to reminisce and reflect, what could your role involve? If a mourner is questioning everything, how might you reply? If a mourner is looking toward the future, what could you say or do?

What to Avoid

As grief care kindred, we try to avoid worsening the heaviness of bereavement. One way that people inadvertently add weight is by repeatedly asking what a mourner needs. Of course, this is rooted in kindness, but those deep in grief don't always know. Their thinking is clouded, and their brain is taxed from incorporating so much change. Trying to determine what would be useful can increase feelings of overwhelm. We'll discuss this more in the "Grief Visits" chapter.

Another way visitors inadvertently add heaviness is by sharing their own stories of loss. Although we don't want mourners to feel alone in their grief, we also don't want to compound their experience by adding our own. Whether it's directed at the same loss or a similar one from the past, focusing on your emotions might lead the person grieving to reassure you. That can be draining.

If it is a shared loss, then you will both benefit from support—from each other and additional sources. If not, then it's important to remember that kindred grief care is about providing comfort, not receiving it. We'll continue to discuss maintaining our wellness and circles of care.

As an important aside, we must recognize that although loneliness can be a challenging aspect of loss, a visit isn't always what's best for a mourner. Whether it's because they're more introverted, tired, or they're overwhelmed with company, sometimes space away from others can be soothing. Dropping off a meal or thoughtful card or gift can be a nice way to express kindness and concern. You can continue to reach out as it feels appropriate, knowing it's up to the grieving person to determine what they need, and when they need it.

Pause and Reflect

Introspection is a key part of preparing to offer grief care. Pause now and reflect on how you've supported loss in the past. Gently assess previous interactions and visits, either when you offered care or when you witnessed support. What would you repeat and what might you avoid?

Using your preferred mode of reflection, whether it is quiet contemplation or free writing, think deeply about these prompts before returning to the guidebook. Remember to extend grace to yourself. You were doing the best you could with what you had available. And now you're expanding your awareness.

When we know more, we can do better. Learning is ongoing. As you encounter new stories of grief—in real life but also in books or media—envision yourself within the scenes. Notice if the mourner is leaning into life, leaning into loss, or needing rest. In turn, how could you respond?

Providing kindred grief care requires awareness and humility. It bears repeating that we can never say "never" and never say "always" when it comes to loss. We can count on this realm to be opaque at best.

This is not a role to be mastered; it is one to practice. Each visit with a mourner will inform and refine your approach to care. You will often need to *feel* your way through, shapeshifting and adjusting to meet each moment, while also acknowledging when someone's needs reach beyond your scope.

Being the Bridge

Having an awareness of grief-related services is valuable. If you're not already familiar, take time to research what's available in your area. Are there support groups? Are there hospice organizations that offer bereavement care? Many hospices extend grief services to those beyond their own clients. Are there therapists who focus on loss? Are there child life specialists at local hospitals who care for young people experiencing grief? Are there camps, retreats, or other gathering spaces for mourners?

Hold this question in mind: "If not you, who?" If a bereaved person has an unmet need beyond your reach, you might research additional options for their consideration. If they're interested in pursuing any of the ideas, you might also make the initial call or gather additional details. Affirm just how vital extra assistance can be during such a difficult time. There are many, many barriers to people receiving the care they deserve, including social stigma, finances, challenges identifying or verbalizing distress, shame due to a perceived lack of strength, or the fear that support is impossible to access.

As grief care kindred, we give what we can without overriding our limits. We present choices and open doors. We praise the advantages of adding strands to the care web and tailor our approaches to each person's situation. Our goal is to help create the conditions that encourage mourners to find *their* best way through the experience, by knowing what's available and tuning into their inner voice.

5

The Art and Science of Listening

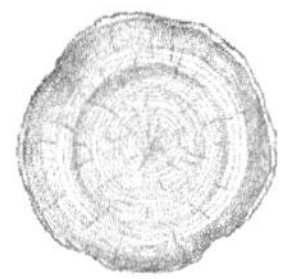

As human beings, we are inclined to question life and make meaning out of its moments—or to at least try to make some sense of it all. It's in our nature to wonder. Following a life-changing loss, mourners often ask, "Why?" Why this? Why me? Why do things have to end? Why do we die? Why do we live? There's an ache to understand. As a species, our brains prefer order to upheaval.

Yet a loss can seem impossible to comprehend. Questions go unanswered. Mysteries go unsolved. The mind struggles to incorporate the ending and adjust to its outcomes. Rarely logical or predictable, grief can feel like a jumble of reactions and thoughts.

Multiple Truths

As mentioned, people can hold multiple truths simultaneously, even when they seem opposing. This is a common feature of the grieving process, but I first noticed it in my work as a birth doula. A few weeks after delivery, I would visit my clients to check on their transition. I began to notice an unexpected pattern. The people I had supported—the ones I stood by for hours or even days as they journeyed through labor—kept telling me their birth stories. It was surprising because I was present and involved the entire time. I knew their stories well; I'd played an extensive role within them.

Eventually, I realized they weren't telling me because I needed to hear it; they were telling me because *they* needed to hear it. They were trying to better understand what had happened, since birth can be surreal and multifaceted. They wanted to make sense of their experience by piecing together the scenes they remembered and asking about the moments that were unclear. As they shared, they were forming a narrative.

Not only did this narrative help produce a chronological account of what had occurred, it also invited deeper reflection. My clients pondered: How was my experience? How did it feel? What did I end up worrying about, seeking, or wanting? Who was I as the main character? Who was in the supporting cast? Who am I as a result of what I went through? What am I still questioning? Regretting? Celebrating? What needs healing? How do I carry all of this?

As these new parents looked back on their births, there were sometimes moments of disappointment. Maybe someone had wanted to labor without medication but ended up requesting an epidural. Maybe they had planned to receive pain medication, but labor was progressing too quickly for that to happen. Perhaps they faced an unanticipated issue that necessitated a surgical (cesarean) birth.

I noticed some clients could integrate varying emotional reactions into one cohesive story, but many struggled to weave together the threads. Was it okay to be frustrated about some aspects of their labor while rejoicing in this new life? Was it "normal" to wish for more ease and joy in the early days, which were more exhausting than expected? Did feeling a certain way make them a terrible parent? An ungrateful person? A failure? A complicated mess?

Questions and concerns swirled. As a doula, I could normalize the complexities. I gave my clients permission to grieve the birth they had hoped for while finding gratitude for positive outcomes. I let them know it's common to have mixed emotions, and for the parent baby bond to take time to develop.

We can examine and hold multiple truths at the same time. It's part of the integration process.

Similarly, people grieving or facing loss tend to *story* their experiences. When a person's worldview is drastically altered by a profound ending, they gradually begin the work of rebuilding perceptions—of figuring out how to *be* within the unfamiliar and unknown. They might verbally contend with or doubt reality, or even rail against it. At other moments, they might find courage to name what's happening and use the past tense regarding life before loss. All the while, they are crafting an account to explain it to themselves and others.

StoryListening

During the peak of the COVID-19 pandemic, our research team at the Vermont Conversation Lab set out to address and study loneliness associated with grief.[14] Initially, we planned to launch our "StoryListening Project" as an in-person intervention before the world largely shut down. With broad isolation measures in place, we reworked the details, knowing our research questions were more urgently relevant than ever.

We invited people who had experienced a death loss to participate. This included friends and family members as well as affected clinicians and staff who had cared for patients. COVID-19 could have been the cause of death or not. After an intake phone call with our research coordinator, we scheduled a session with a trained storylistening doula (SLD).

To open the session, the SLD would welcome the participant, facilitate introductions, briefly describe what to expect, and check in to make sure the timing still felt right for this conversation (that talking about loss wouldn't cause overwhelm). From the outset, we wanted to ensure the storyteller had full agency.

After confirming the participant's readiness, the SLD would ask the opening question: "In your own words and in as much detail as you'd like, can you share with me the story of your loss?" Then, the participants would take as much time as needed to relay their experience. What was asked of (and by) the doula differed each time, but our approach was to be nondirective, responsive, and caring.

Through developing the intervention, conducting sessions, and publishing journal articles with the team, I learned a great deal about grief and connection.[15,16] It was an involved, illuminating project that allowed me to study the mechanics of skillful listening. And now, I can share relevant highlights with you to enhance our study of loss. We'll start with how to hold space.

The Ins and Outs of Holding Space

When we welcome new storylistening intervention-ists onto our team, one of the first training sessions includes guidance for creating a container for meaningful connection. We use a framework from my doula guidebook called the "Ins of Holding Space."[17] Let's go into detail about each component as related to grief visits.

1. Internal Shifts

2. Internal Presence

3. Invitations

4. Inclusion

The first "in" is **Internal Shifts**, which involves slowing down your pace. We're often darting about during the day, rushing from one task to another. However, the energy we bring into a mourner's space impacts our interaction and can have ripple effects. Knowing this, we shift into a more focused, calm state. To do so, we need to set aside our to-do lists and worries, knowing we can return to them afterward.

Developing a ritual for "shifting in" is very useful. Inspired by a Healing Touch workshop, I developed a process of pausing, closing my eyes, and thinking about the endless space above me—beyond what I can actually see, as far as I can imagine. Then I envision the space below me, again beyond what I can see, down into the earth. Next, I find myself in the middle of both poles, feeling more centered. Then, I picture the area directly around me as an energy bubble, which I bring into balance from top to bottom, side to side, and front to back. I am encircled by a sense of equilibrium. This practice can take mere seconds yet makes a world of difference.

The second "in" is **Internal Presence**. This is more about mindset and orientation. We suspend judgment and a fixed agenda as grief care kindred, remembering that this loss is not ours to interpret, evaluate, or resolve. It's ours to support. We enter conversations with open minds, our curiosity engaged, ready to learn from the mourner—and grief itself. We act as allies and steady companions.

The third "in" is **Invitations**. When visiting a mourner, we invite them to grieve fully and freely in whatever ways are needed. We make space for their experience and convey, even without words, "Join me. Be yourself here. Feel safe and accepted here." There's no formal RSVP required, and people can change their minds at any point. We're willing to lean into the loss or away from it, as directed by the bereaved. We are neutral yet available.

The fourth and final "in" is **Inclusion**. We recognize the landscape of loss as boundless and wild. Grief is a process in flux, with shifting sensations and dynamics. We respond with flexibility, allowing everything in. We trust a pathway will materialize in real time, even if it's just one half-step at a time.

After a handful of storylistening sessions, I realized how crucial it was to also "shift out" afterward. When I'm acting as a doula, time often slows or stands still, and it involves a different mode of being. When I return to "regular life," I have to do so with intention, or my head and heart won't feel adequately attached. A threshold pause works nicely. After finishing a session or visit, I find somewhere to stop and catch my breath. I briefly reflect on what I have witnessed, knowing I can delve deeper while writing in my journal or during a walk later. I visualize releasing all that isn't mine and carrying forward the lessons meant for my contemplation and growth. Most importantly, I make sure I'm present in my body and the moment.

As you step into the role of grief care kindred, it will be vital to develop your own process for shifting in and out. What ritual might work well for you? Whether it's humming a certain song, repeating a prayer or poem, leading yourself through a visualization, or focusing on your breath, find what works and use it regularly. We'll go over additional ideas in the chapter on grief visits, as self-preparation is vital for entering such complex times.

Connectional Listening

Listening is part of every interaction we have, whether through sound, observation, or other means. In conversation, there's an exchange—of words, gestures, information, and emotion. *Connectional Listening*—what I'm naming this blend of storylistening and grief healing—is a fusion of my research and doula work. The name was inspired by "Connectional Silence" research done at the Vermont Conversation Lab, which focuses on pauses within clinical communication.[18] The team studies conversational silence as a potential indicator of interpersonal connection.

Connectional listening, focused on communication within community grief care, is not necessarily automatic or routine. It involves skills that can be developed and strengthened. To embody and employ this kind of listening, we must foster a brave willingness to enter conversations without a predetermined script, instead following where the storyteller leads. As such, we follow a framework built around the following guideposts.

Connectional Listening Tenets

- Adopt a stance of engaged neutrality and acceptance.

- Suspend a fixed agenda.

- Cultivate a non-anxious presence.

- Allow and welcome silence.

- Offer validation through receptive, reflective listening.

- Remain non-directive yet resourceful.

- Normalize universal experiences, like loss, grief, and suffering.

- Respect cultures, beliefs, identities, and perspectives.

As connectional listeners, we view loss as natural and also layered. We know that providing company and a sounding board can be a comfort. Equally, we try to avoid what isn't appropriate or supportive. We do not advise, proselytize, or provide medical advice, solutions, arguments, agreements, false reassurances, or therapy.

Feeling *seen and heard* can ease some of the loneliness of grief. In her book, *Kitchen Table Wisdom*, Dr. Rachel Naomi Remen explains, "The most basic and powerful way to connect to another person is to listen."[19] She goes on to say: "A loving silence often has far more power to heal and to connect than the most well-intentioned words."

Silent Listening

Normally in conversation, we fill quiet moments because they seem awkward. We want to keep the exchange going, so we ramble, steal the spotlight, or change the topic. In order to develop connectional listening skills, we must first and foremost be able to find ease within pauses. During training and research sessions, silence continues to confirm its worth.

To begin storylistening sessions, our process is to ask the opening question and then patiently wait as the storyteller gathers their thoughts into narrative form. Instead of forcefully leading them through the conversation, we offer ample time so they can find their own way, pausing before verbal responses in case they have more to say. When we hang on to silence a little longer than usual, the storyteller often delves deeper into a thought or expresses more aloud. Both are essential for accessing additional insights. If the storyteller turns to us for guidance, we respond with trustful reassurance.

During one particularly memorable session, I caught the story of a bereaved adult daughter. She shared that with a few months, she welcomed her first baby into the world and supported her mother's exit from life. As she described having mixed emotions on Mother's Day during that period, she paused mid-sentence. I held onto that long silence, trusting it was fertile ground. When she found her voice again, she appeared to discover new clarity about her inner workings. And she seemed to make peace with the impossible decisions she had been forced to make.

During the listening workshops I lead, I have participants practice silent listening in pairs. It's an illuminating exercise that shows how silence can be uncomfortable. To preface the activity, I give the group a writing prompt. I ask them to reflect on a time when they felt truly supported. Then, I ask them to find a person they don't know well and take turns sharing those experiences. The speakers are to keep talking and allow their thoughts to go wherever they may. The listeners are to be attentive and engaged while keeping any verbal responses to a minimum. Nodding or affirming utterances like "mmm hmm" are okay, but not words. Instead, they are to give the speaker all the airtime. I monitor the clock and tell them when to switch roles.

When we come back together as a group, participants express various responses. Some listeners experience a sense of liberation because their *only* task was to be present, not to counsel. Other listeners question the value of the role and wish they could have done more. The speakers, however, repeatedly confirm how they felt cared for and heard.

This rang true for me when I filled in because of odd numbers. My partner was a young man with kind eyes. When I was the storyteller, I spoke about a tender career transition in my past, sensing I had the space to share whatever came to the surface. During the debrief, he said he feared his role had been ineffective. I explained that because of his genuine attentiveness, I felt comfortable enough to be open and honest. It was cathartic to a surprising degree—even for me, a believer.

During another workshop, I partnered with someone who struggled to share a story. She opened with an apology for "not having much to say." She knew I was going to remain silent as the listener, so she struggled with how to fill the time. I sat back and tried to be comfortable with her discomfort. I tried to exude patience and encouragement, attempting to silently convey there was no need to rush or perform. Four minutes into the six-minute stretch, her words began to flow.

It's disarming to drop some of the tools we regularly use, including verbal language. Although this challenge is prevalent in grief care, I first noticed it in birthwork. Primary partners would regularly tell me they felt "helpless" or "useless" as they watched their person struggle during labor. Conversely, those who were laboring often said they couldn't have done it without their partner—that their support had meant everything.

In service of this fascinating clash of perspectives, can we develop more trust in the value of *being* versus always *doing*?

Navigating Silence

Infusing more silence into conversation takes bravery and a mindset shift. As connectional listeners, we believe in what might be uncovered and reconciled within the quiet. The first step is to allow silence to be an invitation. Frame it as such in your mind. If the speaker requests feedback following a pause, verbally or through facial expressions, take an extra breath and respond with one of the following approaches.

- Nod and provide an affirmational "hmm" or "mmm."

- Thank them for sharing with you.

- Use a validation statement while inviting clarification, such as, "That sounds [heavy, challenging, awe-inspiring]," or "I imagine that was really [hard, exhausting, heartbreaking]."

- Re-word something you heard while leaving room for them to correct your summary by adding, "...is that true for you?"

- Ask an exploratory question, such as "Did you want to say more about..."

- Offer physical contact when appropriate, like holding hands or embracing.

Mostly, you will simply reassure them you are listening and they can take their time.

Pause and Practice

Have you tried holding onto silence longer than usual? Have you allowed a *pregnant pause* to stretch on? At first, it likely won't feel comfortable. It can actually be awkward for all involved, especially if you already have a certain conversational style established. The other person might find it odd to experience a new rhythm. Still, it's worth it to try.

During the next few days, incorporate more silence into your communication. Choose your practice partners wisely. Find people who will be open to it. You might decide to tell them in advance, saying you'd like to try out a listening technique for your own learning. Or you might just subtly allow extra time after a sentence ends. The worst case? The speaker asks if you're paying attention because they're unsure. Then, you can try out some of the aforementioned responses and invite them to explore their thoughts fully.

Balanced Listening

Silence is a vital skill we use as grief care kindred, but it doesn't mean we never respond. After leading workshop participants through silent listening, I follow it with an exercise to practice balanced listening. During this segment, I offer a new writing prompt, and then instruct the listeners to be centered, grounded, and receptive. They are to avoid comparing or contrasting, as well as rescuing or fixing. Instead, they welcome silence but also try to re-word a significant point made by the speaker—an insight, source of strength, or sense of meaning while mirroring their specific phrasing.

By starting with complete silence, this reset to middle ground is appreciated. It feels more natural. That's what we're going for as grief care kindred. We're not robotic; we are kind and approachable. The words we choose aren't scientific or cold; they're thoughtful and caring. Review and return to the following list of reminders as you reinforce your listening style.

Connectional Listening Techniques

- Allow, don't direct.

- Listen, don't lead.

- Leave ample space for silence.

- Recognize and adapt to the unique pacing and communication style of each speaker.

- Notice hidden assumptions you have regarding the length or depth of someone's story or the emotions they convey. It is their choice to share and their process to lead. We encourage mourners to chart their own healing journey, including how much they talk about loss.

- Avoid thinking of questions while the grieving person is speaking. Trust they will arise when needed.

- Try to use prompts in the form of *opt-in* questions, for example, "Would you like to say more about...?" versus "Tell me more about..." This shows your willingness to journey with them through complex topics yet leaves them in charge of deciding.

- Remember that grief has many causes and effects, such as loss of confidence, safety, normalcy, independence, roles, identities, relationships, access to support, and more.

- After a mourner talks about loss, avoid creating a disingenuously positive summary. There's no need to find the "bright side." Let it be what it was and express gratitude for having had the honor of listening.

Tender Shares

Sometimes when sharing about loss, a grieving person will disclose details that are heavy to hear. These intense admissions often begin with "If only" or "I wish." They can include guilt, as though they're holding themselves responsible or at fault; neglect, as in fear they didn't do enough; or resentment and blame, including feelings of powerlessness and frustration. The mourner might also wish circumstances had been better.

When listening to tender shares, you must first realize it is a privilege to be entrusted with such honesty. It's a clear sign that you have been deemed safe and trustworthy. We must also note that, most of the time, people are just trying to wrap their own heads around what happened, so it's best not to get in their way. Instead, we can offer space and time for them to work with unformed ideas and unhealed wounds. Here are some approaches to utilize.

Responses to Tender Shares

1. Humanize

   Heavy disclosures are deeply felt and vulnerably shared. They're a call for attentive kindness. Develop compassion, lean in, and be present. Convey your willingness to go where the mourner needs to go—even toward what is difficult to name or embarrassing to admit—reassuring them that whatever is said will be confidential.

2. Hold Silence

    Remember to hold on to quiet moments as an invitation for further exploration. Instead of filling pauses, cultivate trust in the mourner's inner wisdom and strength. Gradually, gently opening up to the fullness of an experience is the way toward feeling whole again.

3. Acknowledge

    Recognize emotions and insights without needing to confirm whether they are right, wrong, just, or true. Be supportive without offering your assessment. We do not condone or condemn, as it is not our place to judge. We remain neutral, recognizing this is *their* experience to navigate.

Lastly, you can encourage their processing by saying, "I'm a sounding board," "Feel free to vent," or "There's no need to have it all figured out."

Difficult Disclosures

What if a mourner discloses a history of mistreatment, neglect, or abuse? This can be startling and upsetting, but try to stay calm and centered. Do not ask for details. Allow them to share as long as hearing their story won't threaten your wellbeing.

If listening to another person's account of trauma might activate your own, gently let them know you are also actively working to cope. Because of that, you need to be extra careful to protect your ears and heart. Instead of delving into details, you can instead brainstorm coping strategies and additional resources to support the mourner's healing.

If you have the capacity to hear more about their experience, listen to what the person would like to share, and respond with care. Here are examples of supportive responses.

- Compassionate silence while placing your hand over your heart, which demonstrates concern and can settle your nervous system.[20]

- Gratitude, as in, "Thank you for sharing that with me," or "I'm glad you felt comfortable sharing that; it's a lot to hold and carry."

- A kind statement of support, such as, "I'm so sorry you had to endure that."

- A physical gesture of support instead of words, like an embrace, if appropriate.

Act as an ally as you companion them through their share. If they seem acutely anxious, ask what destressing techniques have worked well in the past. Sometimes simply letting them know you'll stay until they feel more stable can be comforting.

If their system doesn't begin to regulate, consider seeking another level of support, like calling or texting a crisis line. See the appendix for resources.

6

Taking Good Care

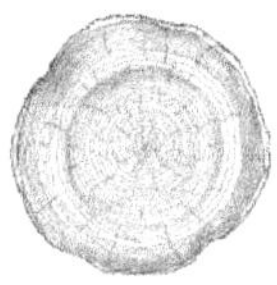

Stories of grief can be intense, especially when a mourner reveals troubling aspects. Confessions have the potential to weigh heavily on the minds of grief care kindred. How can we offer support without sacrificing our own wellbeing?

As discussed, our mindset is foundational. Caring from a place of compassion is essential. Believing in the strength and wisdom of each mourner, even when they doubt it themselves, is powerfully effective. And offering options for additional support is beneficial.

Still, additional steps are vital to sustaining our ability to hold space and care well. First, let's establish an essential promise we must make to ourselves, which is to maintain connection to our own humanity. We must remain aware of our own mortality, tenderness, perceived weakness, and innate wholeness.

This connection to our humanity is constantly in flux; it's not a checkbox on a task list. We flow and sometimes flounder along a continuum. The middle area is the ideal zone where we feel stable and energized. Here, we're able to tend to our needs and the needs of others. The extremes on either end—when we're drained and distanced or too invested in other people's lives—can lead to stress and exhaustion.

How can we aim for balanced and *boundaried*? How can we keep our hearts open and engaged while remaining steady in the face of another person's hardship? It's useful to remember to take things *in* without taking them *on*.

Taking it in

When witnessing difficulty, including surges of anticipatory grief, regret, or frustration, we can safely, consciously take that experience *in*. We can bring it into our thoughts, staying close when others might turn away or redirect. We can utilize connectional listening while giving the person a chance to vent. And we can offer feedback in the form of re-wording or proposing resources to consider.

As we take in what we're witnessing, we might notice personal memories or worries arising, which we'll need to tuck aside temporarily. After grief visits, we can reflect more, making it part of a regular practice of introspection. The goals of "taking it in" are to (1) provide individualized care, (2) broaden our understanding of loss, and (3) gauge our own need for self-nurturance.

Taking it on

Taking it *on* would mean making someone else's loss *ours*—namely, taking responsibility for figuring out the situation and determining the "right" course of action. It would involve solving and rescuing. It could also mean trying to personally experience the mourner's feelings and reactions, attempting to empathize to gain perspective and build an alliance. This can be draining and consuming.

Aim to support, not absorb. Remember, this experience is *theirs*. Trust them with their grief as you offer care.

Self-Inquiry for Grief Visits:

- Am I trying to change or control what's happening?

- Am I being forceful with suggestions?

- Am I sacrificing my own needs to provide care?

- Am I sharing too much personal information?

- Am I flooded with emotion and feel easily activated?

- Am I numb?

- Am I anxious?

- Am I experiencing a sense of dread about grief visits?

Evaluate yourself gently and honestly, remembering that maintaining connection to your humanity is an ongoing effort. After assessing, you might appreciate your current status if you're experiencing inner and outer harmony.

At other times, you might need to incorporate extra acts of self-nurturance, like time in nature or with caring people or cuddly pets, to reset. When caregivers reach the point of burnout, they often need to seek additional support. No matter what, circumstances will continue to fluctuate, so reassessments are necessary.

Signs of Healthy Connection:

- Feeling centered and self-aware.

- Having clarity about what's *yours* and what's not in terms of feelings, decisions, and life experiences.

- Being humble and open to learning.

- Being forgiving with yourself and understanding with others.

- Experiencing a wide range of natural emotions, including nervousness and awe.

- Laughing, crying, and expressing frustration when and where appropriate.

Signs of Disconnection:

- Being guarded, walled off, or robotic.

- Being rigid with an agenda or expertise.

- Assuming you know exactly how a visit will go ahead of time.

- Experiencing uncontrollable emotions or reactions.

- Needing to be consoled by those you are trying to support.

With the looming prospect of disconnection, we each must find ways to remain in the balanced and *boundaried* zone. As you develop methods, consider the following components.

Intention, Action, and Frame

1. Set the **intention** to regularly assess where you are on the continuum of connection. Add reminders to your calendar for monthly or quarterly check-ins. Also, look for signs of

depletion and overexertion, which signal the need for a more immediate response.

2. Take **action** to recalibrate as necessary. You might turn inward or reach out to reliable resources. The need to make adjustments is not a sign of weakness; it is evidence of self-awareness. And it will help sustain you.

3. Consider how to **frame** your thoughts. What does all this sound like inside your head? How are you explaining it to yourself and making sense of it? Sometimes the most effective strategy is to question a reaction and then reframe it. Ask: "Is this emotion, decision, or response actually mine? How will this experience inform the care I provide in the future, or the philosophies and beliefs I hold now?"

And as always, cultivate trust in abundance. Build trust in yourself and your kind efforts, and in those who are grieving. Repeat a mantra to yourself, if helpful: "The humanity in me honors the humanity in you."

As connectional listeners, we act as witnesses to people piecing together their loss—of organizing and integrating what has happened. When mourners try to make sense of experiences, they sift through memories, finding threads—past, present, and future—to weave together an evolving narrative. They're beginning to figure out who they are, or might become, as a result of an ending. Throughout the process, they may even find glimmers of hope.

Grief care kindred create opportunities for this kind of story-sharing to happen. We skillfully hold space, allowing mourners to decide the depth and direction of their words. We reflect back what we've heard about their perspectives and any meaning they've discovered. It is an honor to step into this role, and there is a great need for it in every community.

7

Meaningful Messaging

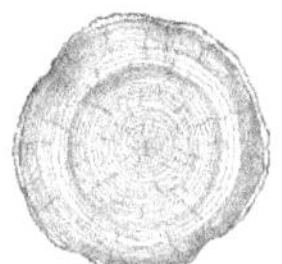

Although we're likely to do more listening than speaking when providing care, it's important to be aware of common grief messaging. In our effort to normalize the various ways loss manifests, let's disrupt some myths and platitudes, and avoid the lure of offering false reassurances. We'll examine some popular sentiments in more detail.

Misguided Myths

- "Time heals all wounds."

Grieving people frequently hear this. It's meant to be comforting—and might be for some mourners, sometimes—but as a "blanket statement," it's not reliably effective. It bypasses any acute pain a bereft person is experiencing, which ought to be the focus. Plus, this statement is misleading, as time alone does not heal emotional wounds. Time gradually enables the process of grieving and re-acclimation to happen. As discussed, healing involves cycling between leaning into loss, leaning into life, and resting.

- "You'll get over it."

Getting "over" a loss is not the goal; learning to somehow live with it is. At first, profound grief is loud and intense. It can be all-consuming, leaving very little space for anything else, as it infiltrates all aspects of a person's being. Gradually, the grief starts to quiet down at moments, allowing the mourner a chance to focus on what's next. There is never a completion or "graduation" to expect. Instead, it's as though the bereaved person must negotiate a new contract with life as an unclear pathway develops into view, one step at a time.

- "Don't move on too fast."

While returning to life is part of the healing process, immediately jumping into a new relationship or hobby in an attempt to evade grief often fails. Any feelings or reactions that have been disregarded or numbed tend to return, perhaps in emotional or physical form. And it's not uncommon for a fresh loss to bring back unexamined ones from the past.

Avoidance can be difficult to witness as grief care kindred, but it's not our place to instruct others how to process an ending. Even though we recognize the necessity of traveling the journey completely, sometimes we're merely planting seeds to foster contemplation. In cases like these, you might voice encouraging sentiments like: "As long as you're working through this loss and seeking what you need, you're grieving. Everyone heals in their own way and in their own time."

- "This is a time of great sadness."

Although significant loss can create despair, mourners might also experience hints of hopefulness. Humans are complex beings capable of complex emotions. People can simultaneously experience heartbreak and happiness, yet they sometimes feel shame for enjoying anything while grieving. It can feel like an act of disloyalty. There might be pressure from others to respond or behave in a certain way while bereaved, or merely a perception of that expectation. A mourner might also grapple with survivor's guilt for their continued living.

In her book, *Me After You*, psychotherapist Gigi Veasey offers this wisdom: "Do not get confused by thinking that holding on tight to the pain of grief is a way to hold on to [your] person."[21] The amount of suffering a mourner endures is not evidence of how much they cared for the deceased. Finding new purpose, connection, and even joy after an ending is not a betrayal. Continuing to live—and even thrive— does not diminish what once existed.

- "Everything happens for a reason."

This may or may not ring true for the bereaved. It depends on a person's interpretation of the loss and their belief in the meaning of life. Grief care kindred do not provide false reassurance, and it is never our place to explain why an ending has occurred. We do not assign meaning to someone else's experience.

Be extra mindful of this because people deep in grief are often desperate to answer the perplexing equation of loss. They yearn to make some sense of what happened and to find out *why*. They're grabbing at meaning to ease their pain. As unbearable as this can be to witness, our role is to be present and compassionate, and to validate their experience. We might respond with supportive silence while allowing the mourner to share. We can also explain the universality of this distress by responding: "It's so hard to understand a loss like this. It's completely natural to want answers right now."

- "Don't fixate on it."

Mourners are commonly alarmed at how con-sumed they are by thoughts of loss. Grief can seem like it's completely taking over their minds. Cognitive scientist and author Scott Barry Kaufman explains that rumination is a sign of "working hard to make sense of what happened...and creating new structures of meaning and identity."[22] He goes on to say that while rumination begins as automatic, intrusive, and repetitive, over time such thinking often becomes more organized, controlled, and deliberate.

It is actually quite normal to fixate on an impactful event because our brains require a system update to adjust to a new map of reality. Neuroscientist and author of the book *The Grieving Brain*, Mary-Frances O'Connor, describes grieving as a type of ongoing learning because it "takes time, can be frustrating, and never really ends."[23] This is why many mourners feel like their person or pet will come through the doorway at any moment. Their minds have been programmed to expect it. O'Connor explains that it's not enough for mourners to *know* that a significant loss has occurred; they must establish new thought patterns through living.

Of course, if rumination overtakes someone's ability to function, it's a sign that additional care might be warranted, such as counseling or joining a support group. For many mourners, simply knowing about this process of rewiring can help them better understand their experience and have more patience. In our role, we can gently share this kind of information to increase grief literacy.

The above "misguided messages" are largely ineffective, so why are they used so often? Mainly, it's a result of social conditioning. Yet when people repeat these sayings, it's not only because the phrases are ingrained, but also due to the worry we feel when witnessing another person's suffering. We want the mourner to get better—to *reach the other side* and be okay again. We want their pain to end. This is rooted in kind sympathy, yet it bypasses the truth that individuals must actually *grieve* in order to heal.

During a visit, a mourner might talk about some condolences they've received, which can sometimes be more upsetting than reassuring. As grief care kindred, we can explain that even with the best intentions, people don't always realize how their words will land. They want to provide solace but sometimes fail to consider the situation through the eyes of the person grieving. You can share these empowering statements to reduce any harm caused.

- Grieving people don't need to believe or agree with every message offered. They can determine what resonates and what does not.

- Grieving people have the right to say that a certain statement doesn't apply to their loss if they feel comfortable responding truthfully.

- Grieving people aren't obligated to teach others how to communicate condolences more appropriately. Their priority is their own healing, not education and advocacy.

Open-Hearted Offerings

Now we're going to review examples of phrases and ideas that tend to be effective. First, ponder them for yourself. Would they have applied to your past heartbreaks? Then, the next step is to decide what to share while offering care. Remember, we do not decipher endings for anyone else. Instead, we offer potential ways to ponder and process loss, remembering that exercising agency while grieving is important.

- Unspoken Words

If a mourner says they wish they'd said or done something differently before their loved one died, it could be an opening for cathartic release. As grief care kindred, we can ask if they want to explore it more: "I know it's not the same as actually having your person back, but if you could have five more minutes/one more day together, what would you say or do?"

If the mourner doesn't want to share the answer aloud, invite them to write a letter instead, which could include sadness, yearning, love, and/or gratitude. They might also add notable (or even mundane) events since their last interaction. They can ceremonially burn or bury their writing or continue adding entries. It's never too late to express unspoken words. Let them know these practices can help lighten some of the heaviness of grief.

- Continuing Bonds

Connection does not necessarily end with death. In 1996, researchers Dennis Klass, Phyllis Silverman, and Steven Nickman offered a perspective on grief which honors a mourner's tendency to remain connected to deceased loved ones.[24] As a result of their "Continuing Bonds" theory, *letting go* and *moving on* began to lose their foothold as dominant messages and therapeutic prescriptions. We now know that maintaining an ongoing, evolving relationship with loved ones who have died is adaptive and healthy.

Grieving people can keep their bonds strong in many ways. Some people do so by holding onto or wearing their person's belongings, like a piece of jewelry or clothing. Others preserve daily rhythms, finding comfort in familiar patterns. One participant at a retreat shared her ritual of hugging her husband's favorite chair before going to bed to mirror how they used to say goodnight.

Preparing their person's favorite meal or dessert on their birthday is a common practice. Some families continue to set a place for their person at holiday meals and take a moment to reminisce. A mourner might also visit special places they had enjoyed with their person or travel to destinations they had wanted to see together, treating it like a "bucket list" to complete in their honor.

Many bereaved individuals continue to have conversations with their deceased. And they usually have a good idea about how their loved ones would respond to them, because their voices live on in the mourner's mind. Returning to neuroscientist Mary-Frances O'Connor once again, she imparts, "I find it marvelous and comforting that the brain does this—creates this physical part of 'we' to carry forever...We interpret what we see, how we act, and our capacity to love, because our brain carries [our person] forever."[25] They are gone, but are also everlasting.

- Conserving Energy

In a thread on Quora about unexpected guidance from a therapist, Kate Scott posted, "Run the dishwasher twice."[26] This simple, liberating advice has since resonated with millions of readers and continues to echo through the internet. It reflects more than a concrete action step; it's a mindset shift.

After people experience a major loss, they need reserves for grieving. How can they conserve energy when it's in short supply? It's helpful to consider what responsibilities a mourner can relinquish temporarily. If this means running the dishwasher twice to cut back on time rinsing, so be it. If it means pulling clothes straight from the laundry basket instead of folding and putting them away, that works. Encourage those grieving to take good care of themselves, accept help when beneficial, and relax high expectations during this season. Conversely, some people find comfort in completing mundane, familiar tasks like cleaning. Only the bereaved can decide what will drain or sustain their strength.

- Narrowing Circles

Socializing can feel like a monumental effort after a loss. Changes within personal and professional "circles" are common. As a mourner's energy goes toward grieving, less is available for friends, family members, and colleagues. Some relationships can weather changes, while others fare poorly. Endings can lead mourners to question and assess their connections. This might mean prioritizing quality over quantity and cutting some ties. These additional losses can be unsettling. Grief is a time to draw near to those who can offer compassionate presence and patience.

- "Opposing" Emotions

Just because a mourner's life has begun to grow around their grief doesn't mean they are happy about it, or that they would choose it if given the chance. Rabbi Harold Kushner describes life after the death of his son with these poignant words:

> I am a more sensitive person, a more effective pastor, a more sympathetic counsellor because of Aaron's life and death than I would ever have been without it. And I would give up all of those gains in a second if I could have my son back.

If I could choose, I would forego all of the spiritual growth and depth which has come my way…But I cannot choose.[27]

Explaining this false dichotomy of "opposing" emotions can be affirming as the bereaved attempt to hold heartache and hope as well as grief and gratitude.

- Building a Grief Sanctuary

In the book *Honoring Grief*, author and psychotherapist Alexandra Kennedy suggests building a special "sanctuary" for grieving.[28] Kennedy describes this space as safe and contained. It might be in a section of a room or part of an outdoor garden. One of my clients had what they called a "mourning corner" for this purpose.

Once a grieving person chooses the location, the next step is to create an arrangement, or "altar," with items that connect them to their loss, such as photos, objects from nature, personal artifacts, or small figurines. Candles (real or flameless) can help foster a more sacred atmosphere. Individuals of any age mourning any kind of loss can design this kind of space for themselves.

Kennedy recommends the bereaved person visit it regularly for limited, uninterrupted periods. That way, they can balance the need for continued living with grieving. They might start by spending ten minutes there, perhaps working up to a half or full hour. Folding it into a daily routine is helpful. Journaling can deepen the experience.

Sanctuary sessions can be an opportunity for a mourner to notice varying emotions, including anxiety, sadness, anger, remorse, numbness, or peacefulness. There's no requirement to change or fix reactions. The goal is to acknowledge them within this refuge, knowing it's for a set amount of time, to help ease the fear of being completely overtaken.

If a mourner faces powerful reminders of the loss during other times of the day, they might try to wait to attend to them more fully within their sanctuary. This practice can be useful for maintaining composure in spaces that don't seem appropriate for an outpouring of emotion. Some people are inundated by their grief constantly, and having a practice like this can gently put limitations on how much time they focus on it. Others feel their grief is stifled and recognize the need to lean into it.

The main point of building an altar is to *be with* loss. As time passes and healing continues, visits might space out. The mourner might rearrange or simplify the layout or even deconstruct the sanctuary, knowing this option remains available to them.

- Creative Grieving

Besides journaling or writing letters, there are many other ways for the bereaved to metabolize and move grief through their system. One option is to express loss through artistic modalities, like drawing, painting, or collaging. Author and community builder, Anika Nailah, is a kindred spirit. The following is a poem she wrote while mourning her beloved. May it inspire your own creative practice.

I can say yes

Anika Nailah

day begun without me
night dead and gone
fear snuck up behind me
looking for a home
I can live in darkness
cuddled up with fear
or I can face this morning
trust in what's out there
beyond the blinds that shield me
beyond this gloom I know
another life awaits me
if I but let this go
let go of what's familiar
the comfort of the cave
bring all the love inside me
the tenderness
the brave
hands shaking
heart bruised
battered
beating
open wide
past these walls
this coffin

I'll open up the blinds
somewhere in all this hiding
I forgot about my light
forgot what breathes inside me
forgot I'm still alive

Another way to work with grief creatively is by incorporating the natural world. Individuals might build a mandala to represent their loss with fallen leaves, sticks, grass, shells, stones, or flowers. This activity can bring into focus the concept of impermanence, especially if the piece remains outdoors to re-disperse itself.

Types of somatic movement, like dance or yoga, are other creative possibilities to consider, especially when grief feels heavy or stuck. A labyrinth—which is an intricate path with one way in, one way out, and no way to get lost—can be a cathartic and illuminating exercise. There's usually a special place to pause in the center. If mobility or access pose issues, there are printable designs available. People can draw a finger along the lines as an alternative.

Before engaging in these practices, the grieving person can set an intention or hold a certain question in mind. During the act of creating or moving, they can immerse themselves in the moment to let things unfold intuitively and organically. Upon completion, they can take time to absorb any insights uncovered.

- Meaningful Metaphors

Some people make better sense of the world visually. If that's the case, you could try describing grief symbolically to see if it resonates. Here are two options to utilize:

1. The Ball of Yarn

    Initially, grief is a knotted-up ball of yarn that's frustratingly impossible to untangle. It's a big mess right in front of your face, blocking the rest of life from view. It's too close to focus on and too big to see past.

    As you tug at the threads, it begins to give way. Sometimes you feel like you're making progress. Other times, it's like you've gotten nowhere. All the while, the ball is becoming more familiar in your hands. You're learning how to hold and handle it. Through trial and error, you realize what approaches are more effective and which are futile.

    Even once the major knots are released, the yarn sometimes gets snarled again. You begin to realize it's just the nature of the fabric. You gradually accept it with less surprise and annoyance.

    Life slowly comes back into view as the once-tight ball becomes a loosened pile. With time, patience, and cautious hope, you might eventually weave the worn-out yarn into something new—a creation with its own shape that bears resemblance to its past form.

2. Transformational Journeys

The butterfly and mythical phoenix undergo incredible transformations as they shift from one mode of being to another. When dissolved into goo within a chrysalis or turned into ashes, these creatures endure a complex process of regeneration. After they re-emerge, built of the same components, they carry the elemental history of their evolution. When a butterfly completes its metamorphosis after relinquishing its old form, it begins again with wings for taking flight. The phoenix, symbolizing hope and resilience, is born anew, reminding us that endings can lead to new beginnings.

We can use these metaphors to build trust in a mourner's strength. We might also gently offer them to others as a means to explore grief. But we would never claim they illustrate anyone's exact story. With any creative approach to grief care, we need to leave room for individual interpretations and preferences.

8

Grief Visits

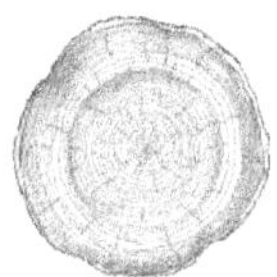

The concepts we've covered so far have established a firm knowledge base. Hopefully, you're feeling increasingly prepared to step up when people are down. Theories and information are valuable, of course, but how do we pull everything together and actually put it to use? In this section, we will discuss just that.

A Supportive Grief Visit Includes:

1. Preparation

2. Presence

3. Practical Support

4. Parting Ways

We'll go into more detail about each component, addressing beneficial steps to take before, during, and after a grief visit. But first, a note about our lens.

The community care model we are using focuses on kindhearted neighbors, colleagues, relatives, and friends providing emotional and practical support. If your relationship or proximity is different (for example, you live with someone who's mourning), you'll need to modify the suggestions to align with your situation.

Preparation

Before extending care, first consider your available energy and explore your inner landscape. To do so, use the approaches we have discussed, returning as needed to the sections on core motivations, compassion, and connection to your humanity. Incorporating sources of inspiration, develop a calming mantra that can serve as a reminder of your intentions and a means for *shifting in*. Here are some examples to consider and customize.

- I can't know exactly what will be needed, but I am willing to show up.

- I offer companionship and presence.

- There's nothing to fix or solve. I'm here to support.

- My heart, mind, and arms are open.

- I trust the grieving process, difficult as it is.

Once you have a mantra or two, keep them close. Besides utilizing your chosen phrase for self-preparation, you can also repeat it silently during visits to reset. Don't get stuck trying to plan the "perfect" words. Start with a sincere sentiment and then make adjustments as needed. You may find that certain mantras work during certain moments. Stay flexible and be creative.

Who are You and Who are They?

The next aspect of preparation is to think about the potential needs of a mourner in advance. People are multifaceted beings, with numerous "sides" and moods, yet we largely remain ourselves throughout life, including during illness, death, and loss. Although being open-minded is key, we can try to tailor our grief care when possible. Honor who you know the grieving person to be while remaining open to adapting approaches.

If you don't have a close relationship, you'll need to be more generalized in your support. If you know the person well, take into consideration their personality and your rapport. Here are some guiding questions for planning.

- Do they have notable likes or dislikes?

- Do they tend to be shy or social?

- When around others, are they more private or openly expressive?

- Are you aware of their beliefs or traditions?

- What can you prepare and bring with you that's thoughtful and special?

Even with the best of intentions, you might get it wrong sometimes. You'll think you have a grasp on a person's tendencies and preferences but be off. If a mourner is able to communicate their feelings with honesty and correct you, it's likely a sign of trust. Remember, we want to encourage mourners to tune into their inner knowing and voice their needs.

Lastly, turn your attention to yourself. In addition to assessing your capacity for care, consider what you are comfortable offering and what role you'd like to take on in terms of grief support.

Anecdote: Preparation

A neighbor was mourning a tragic, unexpected loss of a pet. When I reached out to see if I could visit, she accepted, and we set a date. In advance, I thought about how to arrive. What would I be carrying with me, if anything? I decided to brew some tea, knowing it was a bridge to a place she'd called home in the past. I also packed a few books on the topic of pet loss—impactful resources that are shorter in length, recognizing that grief can affect someone's attention span. I wanted my offerings to be supportive, not demanding.

Before getting out of my car, I *shifted in*, feeling as ready and steady as possible, not knowing exactly what I'd be called to say or offer. I engaged a brave sense of willingness, finding as much trust as possible, as I crossed over the threshold into her space.

Before beginning a grief visit, pause to settle your nerves. Slow your pace and find your focus. Mindfully set aside your own stuff—errands, worries, and past losses—in order to be more fully present. Repeat your mantra. You're entering this moment of the mourner's journey as a warmhearted human being, courageously showing up for whatever they are facing and feeling.

Presence

While providing grief care, you'll address the needs of the moment. You'll shift between quiet listening and helpful action as the mourner decides whether to lean into the loss, lean into life, or rest. If they are sharing their grief aloud, you'll allow for silence and perhaps also acknowledge and mirror back what you've heard, encouraging them to guide the conversation.

Grief Stories

As described in the section on connectional listening, talking about loss can deepen someone's clarity while facilitating their integration process. It can help a mourner make sense of drastic change as they gradually come to terms with it. Some people will speak freely, while others will gaze inward and process on their own. Journaling might be more fitting for some than talking aloud. And these preferences can change. It's a winding journey.

As long as bereaved people feel they have access to what they need, inside and around them, they'll find their way—step by step. You can quietly hold that belief even when they waver. If a mourner wants to share their grief, respond thoughtfully.

- Be invitational, not forceful. Repeating the details of an intense experience can be exhausting and even re-traumatizing. Be open and available if they want to discuss their loss without directing them to do so.

- Listen for the sake of the mourner's healing, not your own curiosity. This is *their* process, not yours. During the visit, your role is to create space for their exploration. After the visit, make time to reflect on your reactions.

- Be a vault. Unless there's an emergency that necessitates immediate help, as in fearing for someone's safety, hold their words and experiences in confidence. Treat whatever is shared as sacred. It is not your story to pass along unless the grieving person asks you to relay updates to others.

Directing Comfort

During grief visits, we aim for a balance of warmth and availability. Our focus is on the needs of the person we're supporting. Yet we are also mortals who experience loss, who are knowingly entering moments of vulnerability and heightened emotion. How can we do so without depleting ourselves?

Hopefully, the connection to your own humanity is intact, and you're assessing it regularly. Still, is it okay to shed a tear alongside someone expressing grief? You will be moved. You will experience awe. Your heart might even feel like it might break.

Tearing up is a natural response and a good sign of healthy connection. What we need to avoid is being consoled by those we are supporting, as comfort should always flow toward the epicenter of loss. Clinical psychologist Susan Silk developed "The Ring Theory" to illustrate this.[29] You start with a small circle. Put the name of the person directly experiencing grief there. Keep drawing circles around this first one, adding whoever else is affected, based on their closeness and involvement. (See the diagram on the next page.)

The person in the first circle can rage and complain as much as needed to anyone else in surrounding circles. Everyone else laments to people in circles outside of theirs. Soothing, supportive words and acts of concern move inward, while concerns and requests move outward. This model provides a great visual for community care. As grief care kindred, we operate in the outer circle, directing comfort toward inner rings.

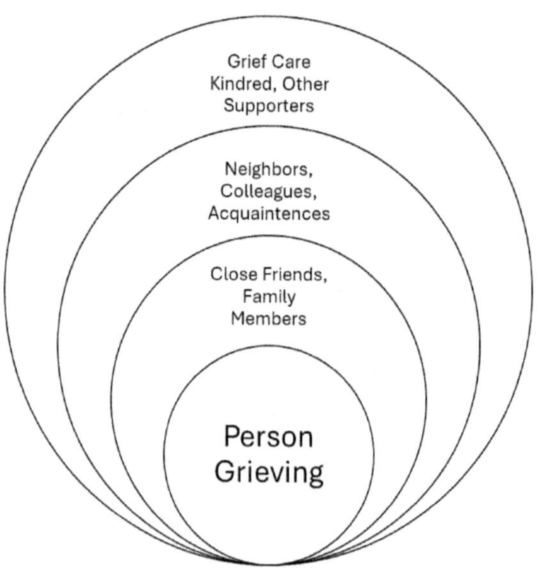

While it's not our place to receive care during visits, we will need a turn sometimes. If we don't tend to our own wellness, stress and unacknowledged effects will accumulate. When I feel activated by witnessing grief, I take note of it in my mind and set it aside, promising to return to it later. Then, I'll take time to think or write about the experience, or I'll talk with a trusted person about my emotional responses. Sometimes I'll listen to sad music or watch a "tear-jerker" movie and have a good, cleansing cry, knowing I need to take care of myself regularly to sustain my capacity.

Pause and Reflect

Recognizing the importance of self-nurturance, how will you give yourself time to release residue? Create a list of ideas that are appealing and actionable. What coping techniques have worked well for you in the past? Use these strategies regularly to counteract any weariness that develops.

Overwhelm

What if a mourner says they can't deal with their grief during a visit? They might describe feeling distraught, hopeless, or lost. It is not uncommon for bereaved people to experience seemingly bottomless, crushing pain or fear sometimes.

Anecdote: Grief Math

> When anxious, mourners might try to compute their grief. They calculate how they feel, add in the time since the loss, and then try to forecast the future. I observed this while supporting a bereaved person following the devastating loss of his spouse.

Because the death was completely unexpected, there was an initial span of numbness and disbelief. A month later, he was experiencing more despair. He had assumed the equation would be grief + time = relief, but it seemed the opposite was true. And it was causing anxiety. I listened and then talked about this calculation, framing it as a question to explore.

'I wonder,' I offered, 'if the shock and practical tasks you had to complete early on helped get you through that period. You were in survival mode. Now, your system recognizes you have some time—and maybe strength—available for grieving. Even though any amount of grief isn't easy or welcomed, it's central to healing. As you open to this pain, you're showing yourself that you *can*. You're figuring out how to carry it. You're building up resilience and your ability to see yourself through it all.'

This client had an internal belief that life would someday, somehow be bearable—and even joyful—again. He was dedicated to seeking whatever support was needed to aid his journey, knowing there would be continued waves of grief to come.

How much overwhelm is too much, though? And when should you consider calling in help? Remember, when offering kindred grief care, you will not diagnose anyone's mental or physical health. Yet it is helpful to know the signs of a potential crisis, including overwhelming emotion, talk of harm to self or others, or acute anxiety. Panic attacks can occur during loss and generally last five to thirty minutes.

The Mayo Clinic references the following signs and symptoms of a panic attack:[30]

- sense of impending doom or danger
- fear of loss of control or death
- rapid, pounding heart rate
- sweating
- trembling or shaking
- shortness of breath or tightness in the throat
- chills
- hot flashes
- nausea
- abdominal cramping
- chest pain
- headache
- dizziness, lightheadedness, or faintness
- numbness or tingling sensation
- feeling of unreality or detachment

If a grieving person has had mental health challenges in the past, they may have established coping techniques to try. If they need immediate help because of acute anxiety or substance use, consider enlisting emergency services or a crisis line. You'll find options in the appendix. When in doubt, reach out.

If the mourner is experiencing deep emotion yet appears safe, you can respond by staying calm, listening, and offering validating statements so they feel less alone in their experience. Applicable options vary depending on the situation, but you can modify the following wording.

- "So much has changed."

- "It's completely understandable to feel that way."

- "You're adjusting to a new life that isn't what you wanted. That's really, really hard."

- "I can't take away the pain, but I'm here for you."

- "I care about you, and I believe in you."

Practical Support

We've covered an array of ideas for providing compassionate care, from connectional listening, to assisting with projects that honor an ending, to gentle explanations of loss that might resonate. Let's review more concrete possibilities.

You will need to consider who you are, who the grieving person is, and what might be beneficial when deciding what to offer. Keep in mind, individuals will respond differently depending on their mood, immediate needs, comfort level, generational norms, and cultural practices as well as how they process experiences. Make sure to adjust and personalize. Not all ideas will appeal to all mourners. The following list, adapted from SpeakingGrief.org, includes in-person and long-distance options.[31]

- Accompany them to spiritual or religious services
- Help with transportation
- Do home repairs
- Run errands
- Bring a meal, dessert, or coffee
- Organize food delivery
- Return other people's dishes
- Bring groceries
- Bring paper products - toilet paper, tissues, paper towels, napkins, plates.
- Replenish pantry staples or toiletries
- Help decorate their home for an up-coming holiday
- Plan a fun night for their kids
- Help organize a memory book or box
- Help sort through their person's belongings
- Help write and send thank you cards
- Give a gift certificate for self-care
- Give gift cards to favorite stores, bookshops, or restaurants

- Purchase stamps and blank stationery
- Bring art supplies or a journal
- Send a care package
- Arrange dependent or pet care
- Wash dishes
- Wash vehicle(s)
- Water plants
- Sweep or vacuum
- Take out the garbage and recycling
- Mow the lawn
- Weed the garden
- Do laundry and fold clothes
- Drop off or pick up dry cleaning
- Set up a laundry or cleaning service
- Make them a custom music playlist
- Go for a walk or a bike ride together
- Do an exercise class together
- Invite them over for a holiday
- Get coffee or a meal together
- Watch a movie together
- Volunteer with them
- Show up if there is an emergency
- Research resources for them
- Help organize bills, taxes, or finances
- Set your calendar to reach out around milestones and special dates

In addition to taking on some of these offerings yourself, you can also use the list as a tool. With the mourner, you can review the options and draft a custom "task list." Encourage them to put it on the fridge for quick answers to the commonly asked question: "How can I help?"

Accepting support is a gift for all involved. Caring people really want to get involved somehow. They want to contribute in meaningful ways. Sometimes, those grieving fear that receiving help is a sign of weakness, but you can explain it's actually a sign of resilience and self-nurturance. Plus, it allows them to save energy for grief healing.

Final Reminders

As grief care kindred, we are not visiting to cheer someone up. That is never the intent—unless that's what the mourner actually wants. Then, and only then, can you juggle, tell jokes, or re-enact scenes from your favorite movie. Remember, you're entering *their* space, and they get to decide how to spend your time together. It might feel natural to follow their lead, or you might gently offer ideas for consideration if they're unsure. You are not there to "fix" their grief or get them into a positive headspace. Show up without an agenda.

Parting Ways

The last step of paying a grief visit is the end of it. Determining when and how to say goodbye requires consideration. Try not to exhaust the mourner. In other words, don't overstay your welcome. If you're not sure, ask if they'd like you to go while acknowledging how tiring grief can be. Encourage them to rest and take good care of themselves.

If you're open to returning, offer that, letting the grieving person know they don't need to decide right then. Are there tasks you could continue doing moving forward? You might also set up a regular check-in time for texts or calls while letting them know responses aren't necessary. The goal is to offer a continuing connection. Your invitations and offers should support healing, not add burden.

You might be hesitant to part ways because you're worried about the mourner's wellbeing or stability. After all, you are a caring person who doesn't want others to suffer. Unless the mourner requires urgent care, try to engage a sense of trust. Your belief in them might bolster their trust in themselves. Grief can be grueling, even under the most ideal conditions. Ask if they have what they need at the moment. If not, act as a bridge to helpful resources. We'll discuss this in the upcoming chapter on connectional care.

Circling Back

Providing grief care is not generally a "one and done" undertaking. If it feels right based on your bandwidth and dynamic, check in again—not only during the initial period of mourning but also on certain dates and milestones that might bring up the loss. Keep in mind that after the first few months, most friends and family members return to their own lives and people stop reaching out as much. A simple "thinking of you" message or card in the mail during this quieter period can help ease some of the loneliness of grief.

9

Children's Grief

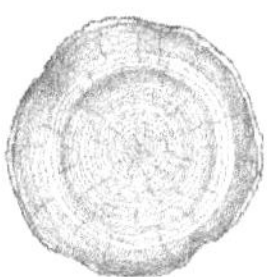

Compassionate approaches to grief care generally apply whatever the age of the bereaved person, yet additional guidance might be helpful to feel comfortable holding space for younger mourners. It's not uncommon for adults to encourage children to be *strong* or *positive* for their family members. This is an unfair ask. They, too, are grieving. They need support and opportunities to explore loss.

In an article about inclusive grief support, clinical social worker Anastasia Taylor explains that children are more likely than adults to experience *grief bursts*—sudden, overpowering and very intense waves of emotion that seem to come out of nowhere.[32] Memories or certain milestone dates can activate these waves, like anniversaries, special birthdays, or major accomplishments.

Early loss leaves a lasting imprint on a child's developing perspective. Whether they're facing anticipatory grief or bereavement, here are some useful tips for supporting children through tender conversations and the inevitability of loss, adapted from the activity book that accompanies my picture book, *Map of Memory Lane*.[33]

• Follow their Lead

Ask what questions they have. Listen intently. Adjust your responses to their level of understanding. Don't over-explain. Check in and pause the conversation as needed. Allow time for processing and breaks for distractions and play.

• Use Clear Language

When talking about the end of life, gently use terms like "death" and "died." Explain how a person's or pet's body stops working (no more heartbeat, breathing, moving, or feelings of pain). Use examples from nature to illustrate the life cycle.

• Welcome it All

Grief—before, during, or after a loss—can cause many reactions, including confusion, shock, anger, sadness, gratitude for a bond, relief that any suffering has ended, and more. Normalize and validate their specific experience and the universality of loss.

• Don't Feel Pressured to Know Everything

Wonder together. Admit that not all questions have clear answers. Explore varying beliefs.

• Magical Thinking

Yearning for the past is a natural part of grief. If a younger child says they wish they could have their person or pet back, it's okay to join them in that line of thinking. Tailoring specific wording to their age, you might say, "I wish that could happen, too. It's so sad that it can't. You really miss them, don't you? Even though it can only be in your imagination, what would you want to say or do if you could have one more visit?" Or you might ask about a favorite time they spent together. In the event of grief because of moving to a new home or school, you could ask what they loved most about the place they had to leave while acknowledging that endings can be hard.

Broaching these conversations is a kind effort—and one that takes substantial courage. This is partly because kids have developed fewer "scripts," so there's less predictability in how the conversation will go. Sometimes a child might not want to focus on the loss. And that's okay. Often though, they'll bring it up numerous times as they try to make sense of what has happened. Knowing they have adults who are accessible and willing to talk can be very reassuring.

10

Connectional Care

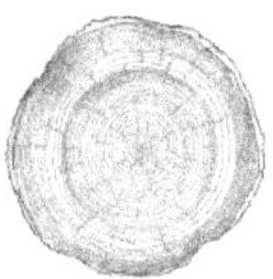

As grief care kindred, we want mourners to feel safe in our presence. We aim to create a haven for healing and a sense of connectedness in the space we share. And yet, we need to balance our kind intentions with the opposing reality that we don't want people to become overly dependent on us. We're not saviors trying to rescue grieving people from their experiences, and we don't want to be seen as the sole supplier of support. That would be disempowering.

Instead, we want to encourage those in our care to recognize numerous sources of connection within and around them, including and beyond us. This is a chapter in *their* story, after all, and it benefits everyone to feel well-resourced. Just as I always nudged birth clients to be proud of their efforts, reminding them, "*You* did the hard work," I hope the bereaved might find pride in their ability to survive heartbreak.

It takes fortitude and conviction to re-commit to life after loss.

Pause and Reflect

Before discussing strategies to achieve this balance, let's come to more clarity on connection. There are countless ways to explain it. When you hear the term, what thoughts, phrases, or examples come to mind? How does connection feel in your body? Do you understand it mostly in your head, your heart, or your gut? Take some time to contemplate this concept.

Components of Connection

Connection is undoubtedly subjective. We each have our own sense of it based on personal impressions from past experiences. And most of us have also known the absence of it. Disconnection and loneliness often intertwine, and both can be present during grief. A mourner might feel detached from what or who they've lost as well as from their own identity. They might sense a distance between life as it had been and the new version that's emerging, coupled with a reluctance to close the gap.

As grief care kindred, we hold this understanding and can speak about commonalities and patterns. And while we would never want to discount or minimize how isolated a mourner might feel following a profound loss, we might be able to help recognize the supportive sources surrounding them. We can explain that connection is a primal need—crucial for healing—and we can note its components.

Building upon my previous publication, *The Death Doula's Guide to Living Fully and Dying Prepared*, here are five wellsprings of connection we'll consider within the scope of grief.[34]

1. Sense of Self

Are there signs of the mourner being connected to their sense of self, perhaps evidenced by an awareness of their emotions, reactions, or needs—either physical, social, spiritual, or psychological?

2. Strength

Is the mourner tapping into inner reserves? Are they finding the courage to lean into loss? Are they reflecting and reminiscing? Are they working through logistics or planning how to honor their grief? Are they leaning back into life and beginning to envision the future? Are they also remembering to nourish themselves and rest?

3. Source

Has the mourner revealed what's sustaining them, whether it's trust in the "grand plan" or the mystery of life, or some other purpose for continued living? It might be relationships that are fulfilling, or perhaps commitments and obligations. What is keeping them *going* through this challenging time?

4. Story

Does the mourner convey a connection to their story of loss? Are they constructing a narrative by recounting events, either aloud or through journaling? Are they working to make sense of what has happened, and perhaps even glean some meaning from it?

5. Support

Is the mourner connected to external sources of care, like a therapist, faith leader, or support group, as well as trusted friends or relatives?

These attachments wax and wane throughout life, and some will be more durable than others. During periods of difficulty, like grief seasons, there are more fluctuations and interruptions. Some people turn away because of a lack of confidence or to avoid someone else's suffering. Others, like grief care kindred, step closer to offer presence and aid.

Beyond acknowledging—and perhaps talking about—the nature of connection, we can also mention any evidence of it we observe. During times of overwhelm, it can be tough for people to notice anything other than pain and longing. They might not see signs of catharsis or realize that sharing about loss and resting are crucial parts of the process.

If a mourner doubts their courage or is unsure about what kind of connectional care to request, you might ask them to recall a prior loss or challenge, like an illness or injury. Gently ask: "What was beneficial? What made you feel worse? What or who helped you regain your footing and belief in yourself?"

The goal of reviewing the components of connection is to better understand their significance. When we realize connection can arise from within—as *innerconnectedness*—in addition to between people, we are better equipped to face intensity. Mourners might discover there's more available to them, and we can find more trust in people's ability to bear loss, knowing they can draw from several wells to replenish their reserves. We must also remember to tend to our own needs as well.

11

Sharing Your Grief

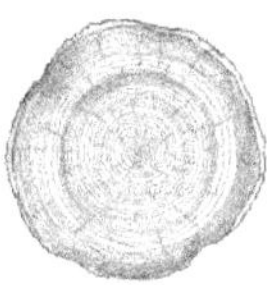

As grief care kindred, we are students of endings and companions to mourners. We are also people who grieve losses. Selectively sharing our personal can be a tool to use. Before divulging our own history, though, we need to first ask ourselves, "What is this share in service of?" Who benefits?

- Are you trying to commiserate or find "common ground" with a newly bereaved mourner?

If so, take caution. Return to the "Connectional Listening" section to ensure you are creating ample space for the mourner's process to be the focus.

- Are you actually in need of support?

If so, you are deserving, like everyone else. But you need to seek care from someone who has the bandwidth to offer it. Revisit the "Ring Theory" in the "Grief Visits" chapter to review circles of support.

- Are you attempting to increase grief literacy?

If so, decide if it is a good opportunity. If it's an educational event or a general conversation about loss, it's likely appropriate. If it's a tender talk with someone seeking your care, it might not be the right moment. Be discerning and check in before sharing. In other words, get consent.

If you decide to share, you then must figure out what to include and how to frame it. This requires thoughtfulness. A helpful approach is to first revisit and review the loss for yourself. To do this, you might talk about your grief experience with a therapist or write about it in a journal. Or you could record yourself recounting the story. Include as much detail and as many of your senses as possible. Consider all the effects, immediate and lasting. Purge it without a filter. This step is for *you* and your own clarity.

You might be surprised by what comes up, or it might feel like a more rehearsed narrative, depending on how much you've spoken about it in the past. The process may bring up other losses or memories you weren't expecting. Be kind to yourself, as you would toward anyone making themselves vulnerable. Healing from loss is ongoing.

Afterward, you can think about how to speak about that loss with others—this time for their benefit. Leave out any intense details that might weigh heavily on others. Instead, use more neutral references. For example, a violent or accidental death could be described as "traumatic" or "unexpected" without including specifics. Remember, your goal is to convey that loss is universal, yet everyone's grief is individual. Make sure not to prescribe what to do or how to feel. And try to eliminate the word *should* from your story.

In service of grief literacy and honoring loss, I will add my own story. The death I'll focus on impacted my life greatly when it happened and continues to echo today. It has shaped my work, writing, and overarching viewpoints.

The Long and Short of Loss

The most poignant loss I've experienced to date was the death of my Aunt Nancy. In the past, I have written about our bond and her dying. Here, I will focus on my journey of grief.

The death of my Aunt Nancy wasn't the first I'd experienced, and others have come since, but it stands out because (a) I loved her so, and (b) it didn't follow the *natural order*. She was young, only in her forties. I didn't appreciate just how young she was until I entered the same decade myself. Also, she had lived so vibrantly until cancer struck. Then, within a few short years of her diagnosis, she was gone.

The short of it? It was impossible to believe. It was unreal. Surreal. And terribly real.

The day after she died, our extended family gathered at her house—the place that was my second home growing up, where Aunt Nancy had fed me peanut butter and fluff sandwiches for lunch. Once congregated, we naturally found our places and roles. The older adults helped my uncle with the logistics of planning a funeral, burial, obituary, and other tasks of closing out a life. My cousins and I made massive collages with printed photos. We assembled the footage of my aunt's imprint while reminiscing about cherished moments.

We laughed and cried. We grieved.

The long of it? This loss has never left me. It's been twenty years since I've heard my dear aunt's voice or seen her smile. Time is fickle in grief—it softens the sharp edges of heartache while blurring the vivid details of memories. Somehow, two entire decades have passed. I'm now nearing the age she was when she got sick. I'm also inching toward the tipping point of living more years without her than with her. This reality is just as surreal.

In the absence of her presence, I've worked to come to terms with this version of life. I've forgiven myself for any words or actions I wish I'd said or done or those I wish I hadn't, knowing she'd love me, regardless. I welcome her enduring presence. My son is named after her. A photo of her making a funny face watches over my desk. When my family eats peas—her favorite—we talk about her. When a Beach Boys song comes on, I'm sent straight down memory lane. When I set or accomplish a goal, I call her close. My Aunt Nancy is remembered.

Still, the world was better with her in it. No one could ever convince me otherwise. And if anyone tried to persuade me to look at the "bright side" of this loss, I'd offer them a knowing smile and a copy of this guidebook in hopes of improving their understanding of grief.

The never-ending task since her death has been to continue on without her here. That is the unbidden challenge: To live with loss. To live beyond loss. To live around loss. To live despite loss and maybe even in honor of it.

Grief doesn't need to be tied up in a bow. As mourners, we don't need to reach a place of absolute peace in order to access healing. Humans are complex beings containing "multitudes," as poets like Walt Whitman and others have noted. We can simultaneously feel bereft and find joy. And we can appreciate all we have while grieving all we've lost.

Hopefully, you will also give yourself time and space to process significant endings. When doing so, incorporate some approaches covered in this guidebook, like creating an altar or writing unspoken words. Extend support to yourself. This will help you become more clear about your own grief and ready to extend compassion to others.

12

Becoming the Go-To Guide

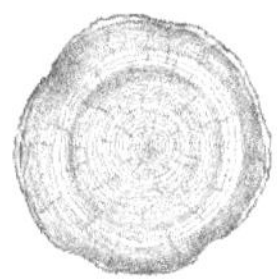

It is a privilege to be a trusted provider of community grief care. It's also a weighty responsibility. As you envision yourself in this role, it's important to consider the potential implications and obligations. We need to be realistic if we're going to be ready.

To start, reflect on what being a "go-to" person means. What terms come to mind? You might cite qualities like being approachable, available, reliable, decisive, and resourceful. Do you see yourself in this way? What attributes do you naturally have, and what could you strengthen?

Consider the level of effort it takes to become a go-to source. It requires having a firm knowledge base—like what you've been building while reading this guidebook. It also involves earning people's trust.

Lastly, it means being accessible when called upon during times of hardship.

As you develop your reputation as someone willing to show up and support loss, you will be sought more and more. When there's a tragedy, your name will be one that people will mention, and your face will be one that people will picture. This can become heavy. Thus, we need to address boundaries and limits.

With honesty, consider your current capacity and availability and ask yourself the following questions.

- When would you like to be "open for business," as in, available for calls or visits?

- When is it *business* (professional or volunteer) and when is it personal?

- How reachable would you like to be? 24/7? During daytime hours? Only on weekends? Does it vary depending on whether the connection is professional or personal?

- How can people reach you? Phone (text or calls)? Email?

Think through these choices and some potential scenarios. How can you set up reasonable expectations and good habits while keeping your wellbeing in mind?

When losses pile up and the call to kindred grief care isn't quieting, you might feel the need to pause and rebalance. Tending to life as it blossoms works well as an antidote to death care. Time in my garden and walking with my dog in nature are a few of my favorite restorative practices. If those activities are not options or they don't appeal, try growing something from seed or taking care of a houseplant. Make sure to stay nurtured and sustained. You'll need to assess and recalibrate regularly.

Haven

It is vital to find where your heart feels at home.

That place of rest and unguarded ease—of unsuppressed truth and delight.

Whether it is in the presence of beloveds, the quiet of nature, the bliss of creativity, or the purity of connection, find it and then mark the path for your return.

13

Endings

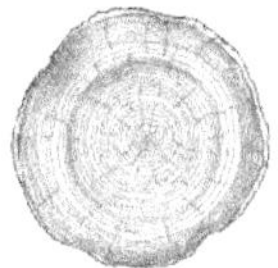

In the end, grief is a natural, multidimensional reaction to loss. The loss could be a death, but people can also grieve a career or role, a prior home, their belongings, past levels of independence, their health or abilities, feelings of safety and security, financial stability, or any number of meaningful attachments. People can mourn a loving relationship or an amazing life phase but also a problematic relationship or period. Simply put, grief is intricate. There are countless variables, including relational dynamics, personal beliefs, and available support.

Most people feel like a major loss makes an absolute mess of life, at least initially. Often, there isn't a neat and organized resolution. Grieving isn't orderly or linear. It's a fraught process unique to each person navigating each loss.

We can't only think our way through grief. We also have to *feel* our way through it, which can be grueling. It can also be lonely.

Feat of Courage

During a memorable "Doula Heart" workshop, a participant relayed an experience that taught the group a powerful lesson about grief. I continue to share it in my writing and talks so others may benefit as well. The participant explained how she had cared for a dear friend throughout his terminal illness. As his disease progressed and the end neared, he noticed that fewer visitors were coming by and checking in, leaving him feeling not only ill but also abandoned.

Instead of taking it personally and passively allowing it to continue, he spoke up. With the help of his friend, the doula, he drafted a note to his friends and family members. "Come and say the wrong thing," he pleaded. He knew that by relieving the pressure people felt for their visits and words to be profound and perfect, he would regain some of his circle.

And he did.

This message serves as a reminder that individuals remain fundamentally themselves throughout various stages of sickness and grief. People are not their diseases; they are *themselves*. They are not their losses; they are *themselves*. This remains true even while undergoing dizzying changes, effects, and perhaps even post-traumatic growth. They might seem unrecognizable at moments, and they will have fluctuating moods, yet we can remember that underneath any distress, they remain whole. At their core, they exist as their elemental selves.

And they need their *people*—their village.

But can we hope for more than arriving to "say the wrong thing"? Showing up is a big first step, but can we improve our grief literacy and learn how to offer effective, personalized support? By deepening our awareness and understanding, we can. It's time to embrace—and enhance—community-based care.

Now that you've worked your way through the information and activities within this guidebook, you will be better able to offer calmness, steadiness, and sensitivity—all told, a soothing balm for a broken heart. Although not a cure, your presence, blended with thoughtfully chosen words and a dash of selective silence, will be good medicine for those feeling lost and alone.

There's a purity to kindred grief care. With pretense and agenda set down, we enter each conversation or visit unencumbered. It is not our role to supply solutions or empty promises. We're not there to make sense of someone else's experience of loss. When visiting the bereaved, our purpose is to provide kinship and kindness. In doing so, we might assist with practical tasks or be a quiet listener. Our main purpose is to help create the conditions that encourage healing.

Though we've covered myriad strategies throughout this text, do not mistake this learning for expertise. You will forever be a humble student of grief, continuously reflecting, recalibrating, and wading your way through delicate moments while making sure to hold thoughtful intentions. This is human work, though, and you are built for it.

As grief care kindred, we are an integral part of the care web. We are the *village*. Now, after studying the realm and trusted techniques, engage your heart and step into this role. You will be a source of companionship through the darkest of times. Take such good care of yourself as you do so.

Appendix

Types of Grief

Adapted from the Cleveland Clinic[35]

Anticipatory Grief

Anticipatory grief refers to the experience of loss preceding a significant ending. It might involve a series of *progressionary* losses that signal a steady decline, including changing roles, identities, relationships, abilities, or independence.[36] In the case of receiving a terminal diagnosis, a person might experience dread, fear, sadness, regret, and disconnection as they anticipate the end of life. They might also feel impending relief, curiosity about death, or a sense of gratitude for a life well lived.

Swiss American psychiatrist Elisabeth Kübler-Ross (EKR), famously known for her stages of grief theory, spent years at the bedsides of people with terminal illnesses to learn about their last phase of life.[37] Her work has been broadly applied to bereavement, yet it originally described anticipatory grief. The most well-known "stages" she wrote about were denial, anger, bargaining, depression, and acceptance. EKR named several additional reactions to impending death, including shock, hope, anxiety, *decathexis* (the process of disinvestment of mental or emotional energy in the outside world), and explained the stages were not linear or guaranteed to occur for each person.[38]

Abbreviated Grief

Abbreviated grief refers to a shorter span of recognizable grief than expected. In other words, a mourner re-acclimates to life or "moves on" faster. This might happen because the mourner has grieved in anticipation of the loss and is more prepared to do the work of integration, or other life demands aren't allowing the mourner space for continued grief. It could also be rooted in a reluctance to really feel the depth of the loss. Instead, the person turns their attention toward something new, whether a relationship, home, job, or life purpose. With abbreviated grief, the loss might be adequately processed—or it might not be.

Delayed Grief

Delayed grief is postponed grief. It's when mourning and grieving happen at a point after a major loss— weeks, months, or even years later. This might be because the mourner had been tending to obligations or other people's needs. It could also result from the shock that follows an unexpected loss, which temporarily freezes any effects. Or delayed grief can follow a period of trying to keep powerful emotions at a distance. Sometimes subsequent losses bring up all that went unexamined in the past.

Inhibited Grief

Inhibited grief is stifled grief. It involves repressing grief responses. This can result from competing responsibilities, including worrying about the welfare of others more than oneself, or can be because of the anxiety of being overcome by loss. Some mourners fear they don't know *how* to grieve, meaning they can't find trust in the process or their own inner wisdom. The Cleveland Clinic explains that when mourners don't allow themselves to pause and feel emotions, "grief often shows up as physical symptoms like an upset stomach, insomnia, anxiety or even panic attacks."[39]

Cumulative Grief

Cumulative grief means enduring multiple losses all at once or in quick succession. For example, a person loses their job and experiences the death of someone close to them within a few months, or someone receives a difficult diagnosis and must move to a new home to receive care. These layers of loss can complicate the integration and healing process.

Collective Grief

Collective grief is communal grief. This might refer to an extended family unit dealing with the death of a beloved relative together. Or it could be broader, like a neighborhood recovering from a natural disaster, or a nation reeling from historical trauma or a pandemic that affected many.

Disenfranchised Grief

Disenfranchised grief is unsanctioned grief. It's when a mourner doesn't feel they have permission to grieve. Individuals or society at large might invalidate a loss by not qualifying it as "significant" enough, or by denying that person's right to mourn a particular ending. This can sometimes happen following the death of a friend, pet, or ex-romantic partner. It can also occur in deaths caused by a drug overdose, suicide, or reckless driving.

Complicated/Prolonged Grief

Any kind of grief has the potential to be complex, but *complicated grief* (also called "prolonged grief") is a more clinical term that describes an inability to re-establish a functional, meaningful life beyond loss. This intense, debilitating grief reaction happens more often in response to disenfranchised mourning, a traumatic ending, or when a loss feels unresolved, such as with a missing person.

According to the Cleveland Clinic, the signs of complicated grief include (1) feeling as if a part of yourself is lost or has died, (2) not believing that the loss has occurred, (3) avoiding reminders of the loss, (4) experiencing intense emotional pain relating to the loss that interferes with daily living, (5) feeling emotionally numb, lonely or as if life doesn't have meaning or purpose, (6) or finding it difficult to live life, make plans with friends, participate in activities you enjoy or make decisions for the future—even after a year of bereavement.[40] Additional care, like individual counseling or participation in a support group, can help a mourner return to living life more fully.

Prolonged Grief

Adapted from the National Center for Posttraumatic Stress Disorder[41]

Approximately 10% of the population experiences a prolonged, impairing reaction when they are grieving. This type of grief reaction is sometimes a combination of posttraumatic stress reactions and separation distress.

The person may feel guilty about their behavior toward the deceased in life, or for living when the deceased person is not. They may fear that they caused or contributed to the death, that they should have prevented the death or that they should have been the one who died.

Prolonged grief can include:

- Emotional numbness

- Difficulty planning for the future

- Loss of identity

- Feeling the future has been cut short

- Retreating from others

- Anger and guilt over not having more typical grief reactions

Mental health treatment can be beneficial, especially when these reactions linger for months, cause significant distress, or interfere with functioning.

The gradual decline in dementia can also spur a kind of prolonged grief. As the disease affects various parts of the brain, the person slowly slips away. In an email to the author, death literacy educator Jana Branch expresses the complexities of caring for a parent with dementia. She shares, "How do I care for this person when I don't see myself reflected in their eyes anymore?"[42] Without that kind of acknowledgment, Branch explains how loved ones can get "stuck in the unspoken grief for what's been lost" and have a hard time seeing the person who is still alive and in need of their care.

Integrated Grief

From the Center for Prolonged Grieving at Columbia University[43]

Integrated grief is a lasting form of grief that has a place in the person's life without dominating it or being overly influential in thoughts, feelings, or behavior. This grief is usually bittersweet and can be helpful in learning and growing in life. When grief is integrated, it mostly resides in the background, but it's often activated on certain calendar days, life events, or with unexpected reminders of the loss.

Crisis Support

If you or anyone you are supporting is under emotional duress and needs immediate assistance within the United States:

- Call 911 for emergency services

- Text or call the suicide and crisis line at 988

- Text CONNECT to 741741 or APOYO to 741741

- Black Line: (800) 604-5841

- Trans Lifeline: (877) 565-8860

- National Drug Helpline: (844) 289-0879

Search HelpGuide.org for global options.

Notes

[1] Desmond Tutu, *No Future Without Forgiveness* (New York: Doubleday, 1999).

[2] Helen Keller, *We Bereaved* (New York: Leslie Fulenwider Inc., 1929).

[3] "The 10 Best and 10 Worst Things to Say to Someone in Grief," Grief.com, accessed December 5, 2025, https://grief.com/10-best-worst-things-to-say-to-someone-in-grief/.

[4] Ibid.

[5] Teresa (Terri) Chaplin, "Some advice makes grief harder, not easier," LinkedIn, February 2025, https://www.linkedin.com/feed/update/urn:li:activity:72954 52813977870336/.

[6] Eluna Network, "Activity: Your Grief is Unique," Eluna Network, n.d., https://elunanetwork.org/resources/activity-your-grief-is-unique.

[7] Taylor Sheridan, writer, *Yellowstone*, season 1, episode 6, "Boring the Devil," January 30, 2022.

[8] Francis Weller, *The Wild Edge of Sorrow: Rituals of Renewal and the Sacred Work of Grief* (Berkeley, CA: North Atlantic Books, 2015).

[9] Jamie Anderson, "As the Lights Wink Out...," *All My Loose Ends*, March 25, 2014.

[10] Kendra Cherry, "The Basics of Prosocial Behavior," *Verywell Mind*, updated November 17, 2022, https://www.verywellmind.com/what-is-prosocial-behavior-2795479.

[11] Rachel Naomi Remen, "Helping, Fixing or Serving?" *Shambhala Sun*, September 1999.

[12] M. S. Ainsworth, "Attachment as Related to Mother-Infant Interaction," *Advances in Infancy Research* 8 (1993): 1–50.

[13] Margaret Stroebe and Henk Schut, "The Dual Process Model of Coping with Bereavement: Rationale and Description," *Death Studies,* 23, no.3 (April–May 1999): 197–224, https://doi.org/10.1080/074811899201046.

[14] Vermont Conversation Lab, accessed September 2, 2025, https://vermontconversationlab.com/.

[15] Maija Reblin et al., "The StoryListening Project: Feasibility and Acceptability of a Remotely Delivered Intervention to Alleviate Grief during the COVID-19 Pandemic," *Journal of Palliative Medicine* 26, no. 3 (March 2023): 327–333, https://doi.org/10.1089/jpm.2022.0261.

[16] Francesca Arnoldy et al., "Protocol for a Scalable StoryListening Intervention for Grief-Related Loneliness During COVID-19," *Palliative Medicine Reports*, August 2023.

[17] Francesca Lynn Arnoldy, *Cultivating the Doula Heart: Essentials of Compassionate Care* (Hinesburg, VT: Contemplative Doula, 2018).

[18] Cailin J. Gramling et al., "Epidemiology of Connectional Silence in Specialist Serious Illness Conversations," *Patient Education and Counseling* 105, no. 7 (2022): 2005–2011, https://doi.org/10.1016/j.pec.2021.10.032.

[19] Rachel Naomi Remen, *Kitchen Table Wisdom: Stories That Heal*, 10th Anniversary Edition (New York: Penguin, 2006), 112.

20 Aljoscha Dreisoerner et al., "Self-Soothing Touch and Being Hugged Reduce Cortisol Responses to Stress: A Randomized Controlled Trial on Stress, Physical Touch, and Social Identity," *Comprehensive Psychoneuroendocrinology* 8 (2021): 100091, https://doi.org/10.1016/j.cpnec.2021.100091.

21 Gigi Veasey, *Me After You* (Hopes Road Publishing, 2022).

22 Scott Barry Kaufman, "Post-Traumatic Growth: Finding Meaning and Creativity in Adversity," *Scott Barry Kaufman*, n.d, https://scottbarrykaufman.com/post-traumatic-growth-finding-meaning-and-creativity-in-adversity/.

23 Mary-Frances O'Connor, "The Grieving Brain: The Surprising Science of How We Learn from Love and Loss," *Next Big Idea Club Magazine*, March 1, 2022, https://nextbigideaclub.com/magazine/grieving-brain-surprising-science-learn-love-loss-bookbite/32708/.

24 Dennis Klass, Phyllis R. Silverman, and Steven L. Nickman, eds., *Continuing Bonds: New Understandings of Grief* (Washington, DC: Taylor & Francis, 1996).

25 O'Connor, "The Grieving Brain."

26 Kate Scott, "Has a Therapist Ever Told You Something Completely Unexpected?" Quora, n.d., https://www.quora.com/Has-a-therapist-ever-told-you-something-completely-unexpected/answer/Kate-Scott-6.

27 Harold S. Kushner, *When Bad Things Happen to Good People* (New York: Schocken Books, 1981).

28 Alexandra Kennedy, *Honoring Grief: Creating a Space to Let Yourself Heal* (Oakland, CA: New Harbinger Publications, 2014).

29 Susan Silk and Barry Goldman, "How Not to Say the Wrong Thing," *Los Angeles Times*, April 7, 2013, https://www.latimes.com/nation/la-oe-0407-silk-ring-theory-20130407-story.html.

30 Mayo Clinic Staff, "Panic Attacks and Panic Disorder: Symptoms & Causes," *Mayo Clinic*, accessed December 5, 2025, https://www.mayoclinic.org/diseases-conditions/panic-attacks/symptoms-causes/syc-20376021.

31 "List of Support Ideas," *Speaking Grief*, produced by WPSU with philanthropic support from the New York Life Foundation, shared with permission from WPSU, accessed December 5, 2025, https://speakinggrief.org/get-better-at-grief/supporting-grief/support-ideas.

32 Misty Jackson-Miller, "How to Comfort a Grieving Child with Special Needs," *DFW Child Magazine*, updated November 22, 2019, https://dfwchild.com/how-to-comfort-a-grieving-child-with-special-needs/.

33 Francesca Lynn Arnoldy, *Map of Memory Lane* (Contemplative Doula, 2021), PDF, https://francescalynnarnoldy.com/wp-content/uploads/2021/11/mymapofmemorylanefinal.pdf.

34 Francesca Lynn Arnoldy, *The Death Doula's Guide to Living Fully and Dying Prepared* (Oakland, CA: New Harbinger Publications, 2023).

35 Cleveland Clinic, "Grief," *Cleveland Clinic*, last reviewed February 22, 2022, https://my.clevelandclinic.org/health/diseases/24787-grief.

36 Arnoldy, *Cultivating the Doula Heart: Essentials of Compassionate Care*.

37 Elisabeth Kübler-Ross, On Death and Dying (New York: The Macmillan Company, 1969).

[38] Elisabeth Kübler-Ross Foundation, "Dr. Elisabeth Kübler-Ross and The Five Stages of Grief®," n.d., https://www.ekrfoundation.org/5-stages-of-grief/5-stages-grief/.

[39] Cleveland Clinic, "Grief."

[40] Ibid.

[41] "Grief: Different Reactions and Timelines in the Aftermath of Loss," National Center for Posttraumatic Stress Disorder, last updated March 26, 2025, https://www.ptsd.va.gov/understand/related/related_grief_reactions.asp.

[42] Jana Branch, email to author, October 12, 2025.

[43] "Living with Loss," Columbia Center for Prolonged Grief, n.d., https://prolongedgrief.columbia.edu/livingwithloss/.

Acknowledgements

First and foremost, to my Kindred Sponsors: Your generous support will bring this guidebook into the hands of so many readers!

- Linda Fraser, in honor of her husband, David

- Adria E. Navarro, in honor of Aurelia Cleaveland

- Lora Olinger, in honor of her son, Joshua

- Dorothy Marie Rizzo

To my dearest friends and family members: Thank you for lifting my spirits and my dreams.

To my early readers: Mae, Veronica, Roberta, Judy, Liz, Rex, Amanda, Christine, Shana, Anika, Pam, Meagan, Dina, and Kathy. Your encouragement gave me the trust to see this project through, and your feedback helped it shine.

To the mourners who have bravely shared their grief with me: Thank you for entrusting me in such vulnerability.

To my lab mates at the Vermont Conversation Lab: Your brilliance and dedication to collaboration is the finest melding of art and science.

To my "Inspired Ideation" co-retreaters: Wilka, Zoe, Shanti, Danielle, Debbie, Hemali, Karen, and Cindy. Your artistic energy inspires my own.

To the Knoll Farm "Better Selves" Fellows: Big appreciation to the "Bread Pudding People" who held space for connection and creativity.

About the Author

Francesca Lynn Arnoldy is a community doula who has worked in the realms of birth, death, and grief since 2009. In addition to *Kindred Grief Care*, she is the author of *Cultivating the Doula Heart*, *Map of Memory Lane*, and *The Death Doula's Guide to Living Fully and Dying Prepared*.

Francesca is a published researcher at the Vermont Conversation Lab with a focus on StoryListening. She also runs the Death Literacy Educator Program, an online course and community. Through her heart-centered work, Francesca hopes to inspire courage, connection, and compassion.

Find more info and special downloads about community grief care at francescalynnarnoldy.com.

www.ingramcontent.com/pod-product-compliance
Lightning Source LLC
Chambersburg PA
CBHW051805050726

47598CB00006B/2434